THE ENTIRE
UNIVERSE
IS A GREAT
THEATER OF
MIRRORS

—ALICE BAILEY

Andrews McMeel Publishing
a division of Andrews McMeel Universal
1130 Walnut Street, Kansas City, Missouri 64106

www.andrewsmcmeel.com

20 21 22 23 24 RLP 10 9 8 7 6 5 4 3

ISBN: 978-1-4494-9186-4

The Book of Tarot: A Modern Guide to Reading the Tarot was
first published in the United Kingdom in 2017 by Ebury Press,
a division of Penguin Random House UK.

Library of Congress Control Number: 2017953089

Editor: Melissa Rhodes
Art Director: Holly Swayne
Production Editor: Elizabeth A. Garcia
Production Manager: Tamara Haus

DISCLAIMER
The information in this book has been compiled by way of general guidance in
relation to the specific subjects addressed, but it is not a substitute and not to be
relied on for medical, health care, pharmaceutical, or other professional advice. The
author and the publishers disclaim, as far as the law allows, any liability arising directly
or indirectly from the use or misuse of the information contained in this book.

ATTENTION: SCHOOLS AND BUSINESSES
Andrews McMeel books are available at quantity discounts with
bulk purchase for educational, business, or sales promotional use.
For information, please e-mail the Andrews McMeel Publishing
Special Sales Department: specialsales@amuniversal.com.

THE BOOK

of Tarot

A GUIDE FOR MODERN MYSTICS

DANIELLE NOEL

Andrews McMeel
PUBLISHING®

FOR ALL
OF THE
MYSTICS,
LIGHTWORKERS,
AND THOSE
WHO ARE
DRAWN TO THE
STARS.

CONTENTS

INTRODUCTION

This book is dedicated to all of the mystics and seekers who wish to explore their own intuition and light. It is also made for those who are new to the Tarot, offering a gentle yet honest approach to its archetypes and meanings. The definitions that you will find throughout the following chapters result from my years of working with this sacred tool (while also being somewhat obsessed with the mystical and healing arts), refined down to a family of keys to help you cultivate more magic and medicine in your life. They have been written from my heart to yours, to give you an easy-to-use, practical guide to this ancient, wise, and intuitive practice. Inspired by sacred symbology, the Akasha, and the fabric of our universe, each card in this book functions as a tiny gateway into inner worlds for you to explore.

Maybe you're at a crossroads, have questions, or want to connect with new sparks of inspiration. Perhaps you've wanted to try out the Tarot but have heard mixed reviews on what it actually does and how it all works. My hope with this book is to bring a soulful awareness to the incredible value of the Tarot as a device for self-discovery—as a confidant, a teacher, or a familiar friend who is always at hand. With these pages, may you unveil some of your own moments of truth while embarking on the endless potential of your journey with the cards.

A SENSE OF WONDER

What I love about the Tarot can be expressed by that same sense of wonder I often felt as a child. When I discovered my first deck, I knew I had a great mystery on my hands. The waxy veneer of the cards stuck together, the edges were frayed, and there was a faint, familiar perfume lingering in the box. This encounter was like unearthing some lost, ancient relic. Up until that point, I'd been the little girl who was constantly in search of a doorway to another world, whether in the form of the rabbit holes in my childhood garden or the dusty, old books in my local library (which, to my imagination, must have contained obscure manuals for time travel).

Over the years, as I became more familiar with the Tarot, I gradually came to learn that somewhere, hidden within the pictures of all the oddly positioned swords and overflowing cups, was the story of my own life reflecting back—that the cards were miniature entry points into an inner world. Suddenly, that missing doorway appeared, and I was able to peer into a new space of sensitive, intuitive nuances that helped me strengthen and unlock my own healing and awareness.

With time, I came to realize that the Tarot was so much more than a simple deck of cards, and, after slowly putting the pieces of this venerable puzzle together, I found myself wanting to create a deck of my own. While I knew there were varying opinions on where and how the Tarot actually originated, for the sake of storytelling, I decided to celebrate some of its more mysterious chapters. I saw it as an encoded language steeped in sacred myth, with hidden clues woven throughout an ancient narrative. I imagined it being carried in secret, traveling over miles of dust, sand, and sea; found in the caves and dwellings of alchemists, mystics, witches, and wizards. I saw its magic reflected in classical paintings, worldly sacred sites, occultism, biblical and gnostic symbols, and so many other sources that it was actually mind-boggling. This was the stuff of legend.

A BRIEF HISTORY OF TIME

The Tarot is one of those mysterious items that has long been attributed with a rich and controversial history. I have always imagined its story preserved within an old, leather-bound encyclopedia, with a century's worth of footnotes filling its vibrant pages. For now, I am going to offer a very brief summary of this timeline, which barely even begins to scratch the surface. This is a story that could take a lifetime to unearth, if you were willing to dig deep enough—which just makes it all the more interesting and alluring.

The very word "Tarot" suggests numerous possibilities as to the deck's origins. There are those who associate it with the Hebrew word *Torah*; the Latin *rota*, meaning "wheel"; the Arabic *Tarah* or *Turuq*, which refer to "four ways"; as well as the Egyptian words *Tar* (path) and *Ro* (royal), which describe a "Royal Path," perhaps translating into an allegorical journey.

The strongest evidence connects the Tarot to the Italian *Tarocchi* or *Tarocco*, which refers to the original renditions of playing-card games that appeared in Europe sometime during the 15th century. There is even a river in northern Italy called the Taro, which may have been exactly where the cards materialized, though no one knows for certain. Perhaps initially created as a set of paintings for nobles, the cards went through several subtle variations while they seemed to grow in popularity, eventually forming the blueprint for what we now know as common playing cards.

Not long after the cards spread from Italy into other parts of Europe, a new system of Tarot emerged in France, in the port town of Marseilles. This was the Tarot of Marseilles, which formed the basis of many later decks. This revolutionary Tarot, rich with esoteric symbolism, reached a new wave of occultist practitioners and shifted the focus toward new schools of thought.

Two key figures who redefined the Tarot as a tool of divination and cartomancy (distancing it from its previous game status) were French occultists Jean-Baptiste Alliette, known as Etteilla (1738–1791), and Antoine Court de Gébelin (1725–1784). Court de Gébelin postulated the ancient Egyptian origins of the Tarot, seeing it as a vast language of ancient esoteric wisdom transcribed by the Egyptian god Thoth, subsequently to be preserved by the priests of Alexandria. Later, groups such as the Order of the Golden Dawn, in Great Britain, developed this idea. Established in 1887, this magical society sourced its information from numerous spiritual teachings and philosophies, such as the Kabbalah, Rosicrucianism, and Hermeticism. Among its members were Arthur Edward Waite, Pamela Colman Smith, the notorious Aleister Crowley, the poet W. B. Yeats, and writers Bram Stoker and Sir Arthur Conan Doyle (to name a few).

In 1909, Pamela Colman Smith was hired by Arthur Edward Waite to illustrate the deck we know best today—the Rider-Waite-Smith Tarot. Both Pamela and Arthur were practitioners of magic and Kabbalism, translating their redefined wisdom into this revolutionary deck, which used colorful renditions of characters for the Minor as well as the Major Arcana and added a whole new mystical symbology. It wasn't until many decades later that Pamela received proper recognition as the artist of the RWS deck, which originally did not credit her name. While most Tarot decks today follow the format of the Rider-Waite-Smith, many have expanded from its language and stunning design, offering an incredible array of new themes and titles to explore.

THE STARCHILD TAROT

The Starchild Tarot that you will see illustrated throughout this book is a modern take on the classic framework of the Rider-Waite-Smith and Tarot of Marseilles decks. It is traditional in the sense that it was built from the major archetypes and meanings of the cards—but, beyond this, it wears a new exterior. The images are meant to act as portals through which readers can connect with and experience their own unique stories and seeded memories as a way of reflecting on themselves.

Importantly, this book can be used with other decks, as you will find all of the original cards in the Rider-Waite-Smith order, with the exception of the Justice and Strength cards, which follow the format of the traditional Tarot of Marseilles. This includes Justice as the eighth card and Strength as the eleventh, corresponding with their numerological associations. The Rider-Waite-Smith order later reversed these for their astrological correspondences, as the eighth card is associated with Leo and the eleventh with Libra. Feel free to use the cards in this book in whatever order works for you.

Some of my cards also have new takes on their traditional meanings. For example, in the Starchild Tarot, the Death card becomes "Transformation," and the Hanged Man is "Perspective"; both new titles correspond with their actual definitions—only in a slightly *lighter* way. The Pentacles suit has also been renamed "Crystals" as a more modern take on its original meaning. This suit symbolizes the physical aspects of our lives (such as home, health, possessions, prosperity) while highlighting our connections to these themes as metaphoric, energetic structures for change. Crystals in this deck also resemble the traditional circular pentacles we often see depicted throughout this suit.

Since crystals play such a large role throughout this story, I have added some correlating gems that align with the Major Arcana. For example, if you were to pull the Lovers card for the day, you could then connect with rose quartz to help further your focus and exploration.

As an added bonus, you will find an extra, 79th card in this deck, entitled "The Akashic Records." This card has been included as a way of shifting beyond the traditional Tarot into a new realm of inquiry. This realm is ancient, wise, and very much connected to how we can access our subconscious in order to navigate new insight through our readings.

THE TAROT AS A MIRROR

The Tarot is nothing short of magic, because *you* are magic. You are the interface. You are the doorway. You are the source and wisdom of the answers you seek. And the cards are here to work with you, unveiling that which lies just beneath.

As a spiritual being, living and breathing on this planet, you are beautifully complex, multifaceted, and constantly moving along a path of endless potential. And when it comes to life, all of us have those moments when our proverbial glass is half empty or half full—when we feel on top of the world or find ourselves moving through a dark night of the soul.

In essence, the Tarot works as a mirror of our subconscious—our Higher Self or Shadow Self—but this is not to say that what it reflects is written in stone. As we become active observers of the cards, the outcomes they point toward also have the potential to change with our thinking. We may look within in order to find the answers and from there begin to cocreate our stories, deciding what is relevant to our path and what is or isn't helping us release, evolve, and change.

At its core, the Tarot reflects the key stages of life, and its language is encoded throughout our own experiences. The archetypes of the cards are constantly unfolding around us: in the people we meet, the pains we endure, the highs we bliss out on, and the greatest loves and spiritual insights we encounter.

SEEING PAST THE VEIL

If you are reading this book, chances are you have heard of the Tarot as a source of divination. These days, it's revered with a much more supportive, lighthearted understanding. Historically, however, the Tarot was often stereotyped as a tool of fortune-tellers and charlatans, conjuring up images of smoky rooms, crystal balls, and someone beckoning you forward to pick a card and reveal your fate. As much as this may seem to be the common assertion, the cards don't necessarily tell your future. Acting more as a reflective tool, the Tarot allows us instead to see how we can consciously build our own futures and envision the paths that lie before us. This potential "future" vantage point of reading also gives us the power to analyze and respond to the subtle energies that may be exerting pressure on our present or future influences. In the end, we each have the ability to discern what is valid and sacred for our own heart. How are you going to write the book of your life?

FINDING YOUR DECK

Finding a deck that resonates with you is a great way to begin working with the Tarot. There are versions out there that are very traditional in that they do not deviate from the established language and symbols of the Tarot, while other decks are completely abstract and seem to have minds of their own. If you can pick up the guidebook that comes with the deck you buy, this will help you make sense of the intention behind its unique language.

WHAT'S IN THE CARDS?

Traditionally, the Tarot contains 78 cards; 56 belong to the Minor Arcana and 22 to the Major Arcana. The Latin word arcana translates into "a mysterious or specialized knowledge or language," which can also be used in reference to the spiritual and physical worlds around us—the realms of our mind, body, and spirit.

THE MAJOR ARCANA

These are the juicy, potent keys in life that shake us to the core and fuel our hearts. Also known as trump cards, the Majors are numbered 0 (the Fool) to 21 (the World). These indicate universal archetypes found on the path to spiritual self-awareness, highlighting stages in life that we might encounter as we search for the meaning of it all. These lessons are traditionally reflected in the Fool's Journey of the Majors as he meets each oracle and transitions through the three major planes of existence that show up in this Arcana:

- ⚠ **The Physical/Material Plane:** The Magician, The High Priestess, The Empress, The Emperor, The Hierophant, The Lovers, The Chariot

- ⚠ **The Mental/Psychological Plane:** Justice, The Hermit, The Wheel of Fortune, Strength, The Hanged Man, Death, Temperance

- ⚠ **The Spiritual/Astral Plane:** The Devil, The Tower, The Star, The Moon, The Sun, Judgment, The World

These connect to the journey of our spirit and the powerful forces that come into play. When these cards show up in readings, it is important to pay attention. Cards in the Major Arcana act as signposts for events, energies, or people that are, or will be, significant in your life and story.

THE MINOR ARCANA

These are the important minutiae of our journey that support the larger, overarching themes of the Major Arcana. In these Minors, there are 56 cards that are divided into four main suits: Pentacles (aka Crystals), Swords, Wands, and Cups. Each suit represents a specific theme within your life, is connected to an element (Earth, Air, Fire, Water), and is numbered 1 (the ace) to 10. Cards 11 to 14 of each suit are the court cards. While the Major Arcana represent strong, long-term, or deeply rooted themes, the Minor Arcana tap into the lighter aspects of the day-to-day arena. The suits connect to the thoughts and feelings we experience and the relationships we have with others.

SWORDS (Air) (Mental):

The Swords rule the power of the mind and our internal ethical principles. They identify our ego, as well as our destructive actions or tendencies. Swords may represent turmoil or power struggles within our life or with others. Aspects of reason, change, or intellect may surface with this suit. The element of Air is projective, dynamic, and transitional.

PENTACLES (Crystals) (Earth) (Physical):

The Pentacles rule the physical realm and deal with issues that involve security and material concerns. Aspects of home, health, possessions, wealth, or prosperity may be highlighted. The element of Earth is grounding, nurturing, and stable.

WANDS (Fire) (Spiritual):

The Wands rule our creativity, confidence, and determination throughout life. They are related to our ambitions and dreams and connect to our spiritual nature and Higher Self. The element of Fire is transformative, expansive, and inventive.

CUPS (Water) (Emotional):

The Cups rule our emotions and deal with love and spiritual consciousness. They tap into our subconscious mind, psychic abilities, relationships, and internal forces. The element of Water is mutable and ever changing, which reflects the flow of our emotions and feelings.

COURT CARDS

The court cards form cards 11 to 14 of each suit in the Minor Arcana and are represented by the characters of the Page, Knight, Queen, and King. Typically, the court cards are symbolic of people in our lives; however, they may also highlight aspects of our own personalities, whether these are subconscious or expressed—like that little voice that often whispers from within or a specific persona you may take on under certain circumstances.

Traditionally, the imagery used for court cards and characters in the Major Arcana is gendered, which is why these cards are very often quite complex to read. Although you may choose to associate the cards with specific genders, the Tarot does not need to be viewed through a gender-binary lens. For instance, a Knight may be seen as adventurous and risk taking yet need not always refer to a person who is male, just as a King is not always male, nor a Queen female.

I have always regarded the courts as metaphors for traits or personas within my readings. To do this, you just need to look to the surrounding cards to make sense of it all. Finding a consistent method of interpreting these cards will ultimately be up to you—perhaps by picking up on their inherent qualities as they relate to the people you know or to yourself. To help shed light on some of the energies and qualities associated with the court cards, here are a few more insights into their characteristics:

THE WANDS

Correspond with:

Aries, Leo, Sagittarius

The Fire Element

Ambitious, Inspirational, Innovative, Exuberant, Impulsive

The Wands are inspired by the world around them. As a result, many of them love to travel and explore. Wands are highly charismatic and self-determined, and they take their life goals very seriously. They have strong leadership qualities and are extremely outgoing, attracting like-minded people. Their beliefs and opinions are in many ways connected to their spirituality, which they consider very important in defining who they are. Wands can sometimes be harsh or fiery if they become agitated or frustrated. Overconfidence can lead to egotism, impatience, foolish risk taking, or insensitivity to others. The aid of other elements can help diffuse the hotheaded disposition of this type. Sometimes, all the Wands may need is a grounding conversation with a good friend.

THE CUPS

Correspond with:

Pisces, Cancer, Scorpio

The Water Element

Psychic, Mysterious, Dramatic, Melancholic, Inventive

The Cups are ruled by the heart. Plain and simple. With this attachment comes sensitivity in all aspects of emotion, psychic awareness, and perception. Intimacy is extremely important to this type in all relationships, whether platonic or romantic. The

Cups want to connect deeply with the people they care about and can sometimes overanalyze others' opinions or actions. Cups are intelligent dreamers and can spend a huge amount of time visualizing or wanting to escape from the stress of the real world. When they are not harnessing their creativity properly, they become prone to sadness, flakiness, or emotional detachment. Cups are creative and artistic and love to express themselves in all areas of their life. They are extremely compassionate, empathetic individuals who are nurturing and caring toward others.

THE SWORDS
Correspond with:

Gemini, Libra, Aquarius

The Air Element

Analytical, Curious, Inflexible, Honest, Discerning

The Swords are ruled by the mind. Their powers of perception make them good communicators, as they are also highly analytical and decisive. As natural intellectuals, they absorb information easily and want to learn as much as they can about the topics that interest them. The Swords are often very good at giving people advice, as they cut straight to the point without holding back. They are driven by justice, truth, reason, and logic, which can make them appear insensitive to others. On a darker note, Swords may be prone to being dishonest in order to control situations or people. When their energies are being used in positive, loving ways, however, there is nothing they cannot accomplish. Swords make strong, loving, and loyal friends.

△

THE PENTACLES (CRYSTALS)

Correspond with:

Taurus, Virgo, Capricorn

The Earth Element

Cautious, Stable, Practical, Conventional, Generous

The Pentacles (who appear as Crystals in this book) are ruled by practicality and strength. They weigh the pros and cons of each situation and always try to take the most logical approach. They are extremely grounded and embody a strong sense of self, which makes them loving and loyal friends. The Pentacles are sensible, pragmatic individuals who work hard at what they do while also making time to enjoy life's simple luxuries. They can sometimes become more concerned with the external, physical aspects of their existence and neglect to connect with their spiritual nature. For many of them, however, this connection is made through being outdoors and exploring the earth. Pentacles are constantly inspired by the world around them, which helps them harness their creativity. Their high hopes and aspirations can, at times, take over the other areas of their lives, which may leave them feeling drained and pessimistic if their plans do not work out.

PREPARING TO READ THE CARDS

how to acctivate?

YOUR HIGHER SELF

Throughout this book, you will notice references to the Higher Self. This is an energy that connects with each of us in various ways but which is essentially you in your highest form. When you tap into the loving guidance of your Higher Self, you may be more aware of visions, synchronistic events, or feelings that let you know you are on the right path. The Higher Self whispers, speaks, or calls out through that inner voice that helps you set your internal compass. It also helps you align with your biggest and brightest dreams.

With the emergence of your Higher Self, you may have bursts of inspiration and ideas or increasingly find yourself in the right place at the right time. In acknowledging this light, and being mindful of your heart, you may find that wonderful things begin to happen.

YOUR SHADOW SELF

When we are born, we have not yet built our Shadow Self. However, as we grow, we eventually accumulate facets of the identities that define us, and, in the process, our shadows and egos are created. These generally begin to evolve as we learn to judge and analyze everything around us: what is good, bad, right, or wrong, and what we consider valid and sacred in life. Our Shadow Selves can be influenced by our family of origin, our societal conditioning, or other external pressures. Over time, blockages within us may occur, preventing us from aligning with our higher awareness or dreams. In order to bring these to light, we can delve into "shadow work"—a concept coined by the renowned psychologist Carl Jung—exploring the suppressed impulses, ideas, desires, feelings, traits, gifts, talents, or belief systems that we have either consciously or unconsciously hidden within ourselves.

Typically, we think of the shadow as the definition of our negative traits, but it can also have positive qualities. For example, if there are dreams or inner creative urges that we have never had a chance to explore due to external forces in our life, these can be illuminated through shadow work. When we do shadow work, we peel back the layers of our judgments about others and ourselves and explore the inner depths of who we are. When we use the Tarot, we can work with our Shadow Selves in order to bring light and clarity to the hidden corners of our hearts, where certain aspects of ourselves are waiting to be reintegrated into our lives. The reversed meanings of the cards can also offer insight into these areas, making space for inner healing and new revelations.

ASKING THE CARDS

As you prepare to read your cards, take some time to quiet your mind and relax. This is an essential part of the reading process, as it allows you to collect your thoughts while extending your energy to the cards. You may use this as an opportunity to call upon your guides or ancestors, connect with source energy, or whatever works for you. As you are the conduit or channel for the reading, it is helpful to feel centered and grounded before you begin, whether you are reading for yourself or for someone else.

Focus your intention on what you would like to address, either in the form of a question or by infusing your energy into the cards as you shuffle. It's a good idea to avoid yes-or-no inquiries and ask open questions, such as, "What do I need guidance with at this time?" or "How can I reflect on my present situation?"

Once you feel that your energy has been worked through the deck, you may prepare to begin your reading. Some readers know instinctively when it is time to begin, while others may feel a warm, tingling sensation in their hands.

SHUFFLING

There are many different methods of shuffling. There is the typical shuffling-and-cutting way used for playing cards, the mix-them-all-over-the-floor way, or the hand-over-hand method, which involves mixing the cards from side to side. One great method I love to use involves shuffling the cards while meditating on a question or feeling. The deck is then opened up at random, much like flipping open a book at any given page. The card in your dominant hand, facing upward, will very often indicate an important meaning. This is a great way of doing a quick one-card pull.

Sometimes when you are shuffling, you may notice a card slip out or find that one falls to the ground unexpectedly. These types of occurrences can indicate an important message for you in the cards, so it is worth listening to your intuition if you find this happening to you—perhaps a particular issue needs your attention.

THE FIRST STEP

Some people like to cut the deck into three piles, then intuitively place them back together again, while others use the entire deck after they have shuffled the cards. It's all about what feels right to you. Pull the top card from the deck; from here, you may continue to work from this pile, or you can shuffle each time you place a new card down. There are a variety of spreads that can be used for readings. Two of the most popular are the Three-Card Draw and Celtic Cross (pages 194 and 196).

REVERSED CARDS

You will notice that the reversed meanings for the cards are included in this book. Many Tarot readers choose not to use reversed interpretations, which works just as well. I have always found it helpful to listen to my intuition when deciding whether a card is reversed. You can also look to the surrounding cards in your reading for guidance.

When doing a Tarot spread, you may become aware of a collective energy stemming from each card in the layout. This is how we pick up on the vibe or feeling of a reading. The overall layout is, therefore, a configuration of energetic factors relating to your underlying situation or question. These energies can shift as you work through the action of shuffling or handling your cards. When a card is upright, the energy may very well be active and manifesting within the reading or your given situation. When a card is reversed, the energy may be in an undeveloped or early stage. Reversed cards can counsel us to unblock certain energies that may need to be released. They shed new light on the upright meanings and can provide clarification, leading to positive solutions. I like to think of them as opportunities for change.

CLEANSING YOUR CARDS

Tarot cards can be highly charged tools, so it's helpful to cleanse them every once in a while to remove any lingering energies and refresh your deck. There are lots of fun ways to do this, such as smudging with sage, placing your cards out in the sun or moonlight, or by doing a simple visualization of cleansing white light. Try to find a method that feels right for you.

THE
MAJOR
ARCANA

THE FOOL
(STARSEED)

Keys: new beginnings • Inner Child • adventure • faith
• impulse • movement • freedom

STARSEED

At the precipice of a new journey into the great unknown, a light begins to stir within the heart of its seeker. This is a seed of inspiration, a thought that has birthed a new beginning—a call for action and adventure beyond the realm of her current understanding. It is an intuitive force that propels the Fool, shown here as Starseed, toward a sacred path of self-discovery, despite the voices of her surrounding naysayers. Feeling at peace with the universe, she trusts it will provide her with exactly what she needs. Poised at the edge of endless possibility, she leaps into the great void.

⚠ **Astrological:** Uranus, Earth
⚠ **Gemstones:** Azurite, Chrysoprase, Chrysocolla, Moldavite

THE MESSAGE

The Fool, or Starseed, is that inner spark of your being that journeys throughout the many lifetimes, forms, and worlds of your story. It is a forceful energy that gives you the strength and foresight to go your own way along a new, uncharted path. When you connect with this part of yourself, the serendipitous moments seem to continuously unfold around you and magic is present in your life. The lessons that shape and form you throughout all of your adventures and awakenings are going to be essential to your self-discovery, but don't forget: The limitations of the outside world also have the power to distract us from our higher calling. This is when we must look inward to find the answers. To seek out who we really are, beyond what we have been told or expected to be—to find out what fulfills us from a much deeper place of spirit.

QUESTIONS TO ASK

⚠ How am I going to write the book of my life?

⚠ What deeper spiritual awakenings are beginning to stir within me?

⚠ Am I ready to take the next big step?

REVERSED

This could indicate a time of confusion or uncertainty over life-altering decisions. If you have had difficulties in making choices in the past or have relied on the reassurance or direction of others, you may want to take a step back, spend some time alone, and meditate on this for yourself. It is important to trust your instincts and intuition at this time. If you are feeling disconnected from your Higher Self, try exploring avenues of meditation, creative visualization, and self-expression.

THE MAGICIAN

Keys: originality • inspiration • skill • direction • magic • power • action • manifestation

THE MAGICIAN

Shown here seated at the base of an ancient sacred site, the Magician basks in her surroundings, the fusion of cosmic teachings as above and the elements so below. From this meditative space she acts as a conduit for the wisdom of the universe—a direct link between the higher realms of knowledge and the earthly plane around her. She is a creative force who knows no limitations. At her side rest the tools of her trade: a Wand, Sword, Cup, and Crystal—representations of all four suits of the Tarot, together defining an alchemical merging of elemental forces, the ultimate marriage of universal power.

△ **Astrological:** Mercury, Sirius
△ **Gemstones:** Apophyllite, Black Tourmaline, Moldavite

THE MESSAGE

As card number 1 of the deck, the Magician represents new beginnings and sparks of inspiration and invention. Your next step may require self-discipline and planning, but, with a dash of perseverance and a little bit of foresight, anything is possible with the power of the Magician. This card also describes the self-mastery that comes from exploring talents and skills, prompting you to find a healthy and comfortable balance in your higher faculties, each of which is associated with a key aspect of yourself: the physical (Earth), mental (Air), spiritual (Fire), and emotional (Water) powers. When working together harmoniously, these energies allow you to channel your full potential—when your efforts yield super-positive results and the world seems full of possibilities!

QUESTIONS TO ASK

⚠ How can I identify where my true skills lie?

⚠ How can I maintain an overall balance in my life?

⚠ Am I ready to ride this creative wave?

REVERSED

Reversed, the Magician may indicate a state of detachment from achieving your goals or understanding where your true potential lies. You may not be able to identify what you are capable of if you are using your skills for negative reasons or if you have not been honoring your heart's intentions. It may be a good time to build a foundation of support for your dreams and aspirations in order to manifest them with confidence and ease.

THE HIGH PRIESTESS

Keys: wisdom • intuition • mystery • magic • serenity
• secret knowledge • Akashic Records

THE HIGH PRIESTESS

The High Priestess is a gatekeeper of deep mysteries and hidden truths. She is Isis, Persephone, Artemis, Mary, Hathor, and an embodiment of the initiates and goddesses of the ages. Above her head radiate the secrets of the cosmos and the ancient cyclical magic of the moon and triple Goddess, calling forth the inherent wisdom of the Divine Feminine. In her hand, she holds a crystal—an energetic structure that contains the entirety of the knowledge that she preserves. Perhaps it reflects the Akashic Records, a lens into the pages of the Book of Life, a vessel for the spiritual revelations and occult teachings passed down throughout the ages. Sitting quietly, she waits in perfect love and perfect trust.

⚠ **Astrological:** The Moon

⚠ **Gemstones:** Kyanite, Lapis Lazuli, Moonstone

THE MESSAGE

The High Priestess is a reminder that we each contain within us the wisdom that we seek. She describes a deep understanding of the higher realms of consciousness and acknowledges the universal balance of light and dark energies. As card 2 of the Major Arcana, she represents a strong duality and internal strength in comparison with the more extroverted energy of the previous card, the Magician, who exerts a more active force. The High Priestess has learned and absorbed the powers of the Magician and now draws upon the knowledge she has received. This card indicates an awakened spiritual or psychic awareness and encourages you to make time for introspection and meditation. It also highlights the reclaiming of personal power, when your own intuitive foresight helps you navigate through any challenges you may have. It marks an understanding of your highest purpose and potential through attaining a balance between your physical and spiritual self: mind, body, and spirit. Trust your inner voice—it will reveal the secrets of your higher calling.

QUESTIONS TO ASK

⚠ How can I access the sacred wisdom and teachings of the universe?

⚠ What deeper messages are being shared through my intuition and dreams?

⚠ How can I connect with my greater soul purpose in life?

REVERSED

It may be a good idea to spend some time alone in order to meditate and explore the realms of your consciousness. Think about how you can take the pressure off yourself at this time. Sometimes, the external forces of the world can be chaotic and draining; therefore, it is important to step back and reconnect with activities you love and enjoy. Reversed, this card may also indicate a harbored secret or truth that wants to come out. If there is something weighing on your conscience, now would be a good time to address this delicately.

THE EMPRESS

Keys: creativity • expression • pleasure • fertility • Mother Nature • Goddess • Divine Feminine • abundance

THE EMPRESS

The Empress stands within an opulent garden. Ruled by Venus, she embodies the potent energies of creation, fertility, and sensuality. She is the ultimate feminine archetype: the earthly presence of both the ancestral and divine mother and the intelligent design behind true creation and transmutation. Her card marks a progression from the High Priestess, merging their combined wisdom in the space of the physical world. As card 3, she represents the balanced magic of this sacred feminine number: the Triquetra; the triple Goddess: the Maiden, Mother, and Crone; the bountiful celebration of mind, body, and spirit.

⚠ **Astrological:** Venus
⚠ **Gemstones:** Carnelian, Rose Quartz, Turquoise

THE MESSAGE

This card often highlights new feelings of inner spiritual growth, developing ideas, or a renewed sensuality. The Empress encourages us to reconnect with our gentle nature and Divine Feminine energy in order to celebrate our strength and beauty. Through cultivating a practice of deeper self-reflection, we may also uncover new tools for personal growth and transformation in the process, allowing us to explore what truly inspires us in life. When we align with this magic, our spirit is strong and creativity blossoms from our heart. The Empress has woven her nurturing wisdom throughout the cycles, seasons, and earthly gifts and asks us to strengthen our vital connection with this knowledge by stimulating our unity with nature and the outdoors. This promotes calmness, increases our energy, and normalizes our natural biological rhythms with Mother Gaia.

QUESTIONS TO ASK

⟁ Am I taking the time to connect with my true path?

⟁ Am I able to ground myself and be present in nature?

⟁ What am I cultivating now in my life?

REVERSED

The Empress reversed may indicate the existence of low energy or a blockage of ideas and creative expression. A need to utilize your skills and resources in order to manifest more harmony in your life. It may also indicate indecisiveness or struggling in a relationship or an overall sense of limbo in which you are searching to find a solution to a problem. Something seems to be missing; perhaps there is a need for introspection in order to question your priorities and soul callings.

THE EMPEROR

Keys: stability • action • success • authority • balance • structure
• reason • protection • discipline

THE EMPEROR

The Emperor sits calmly, holding space for the dominion that he has built.

It is a place of order and stability—a great realm of symmetry, balance, and universal structure. There is a strength in his character; here, he is represented in the form of a large feline from another world—a protective spirit who warns each traveler of the path ahead. If you stick with his approach to life, the journey will be controllable and safe. But be warned, this will take discipline and action. As the energetic counterpart to the Empress, the Emperor channels her creative, mutable power and transforms it in tangible, practical ways.

⚠ **Astrological:** Aries, Jupiter
⚠ **Gemstones:** Aragonite, Jasper, Labradorite

THE MESSAGE

While this card points to being able to strategize and plan ahead, perhaps in the guise of time management and structured routines and responsibilities, the Emperor also encourages us to take stock of our state of mind and powers of discernment. If you are experiencing stress due to external influences in your life, now may be a good time to maintain your focus on the task ahead and reassess how you are processing your thoughts. Very often when our minds are buzzing with clutter, our external world can end up being a bit chaotic and draining. The Emperor asks us to step up and be confident in who we are. He encourages us to take back our power and to distinguish thoughts and actions that are damaging or aggressive from those that are nurturing and positive. From here, we can begin to create order out of chaos and be systematic with our plan of attack. Now is the time to be a strategic thinker in order to get things done!

QUESTIONS TO ASK

⚠ How can I take the initiative in order to manifest my goals?

⚠ What steps will I need to take from here on?

⚠ Where do my strengths lie?

REVERSED

When reversed, the Emperor could indicate a rigid or stubborn mindset, which might be associated with someone who is overbearing and authoritative or who lacks an inner spiritual connection. If you are seeking a more flexible and nonconformist lifestyle, now may be the time to speak your truth and break away from any limitations that have been imposed on you. You might need to detach from certain people in your life in order to heal from within and make positive changes.

THE HIEROPHANT

Keys: counsel • teacher • conduit • community • spiritual wisdom • guidance • knowledge • education • unity

THE HIEROPHANT

The Hierophant exists as an energetic force with many different faces; she is a great catalyst for change, providing us with new insights that help us to grow into the greatest versions of ourselves. Here, a crystal rests in her hand, similar to that of the High Priestess. She presents this offering to us as a new experience or adventure. She is the ultimate teacher and can show up in various forms: in the mentors who cross our paths and the religious or spiritual philosophies we choose to align with. She manifests at different times in our lives when certain experiences may be pertinent to our growth.

△ **Astrological:** Taurus

△ **Gemstones:** Hematite, Lapis Lazuli, Lemurian Quartz

THE MESSAGE

The Hierophant typically shows up when you are ready to expand your awareness, meet new people, or gain fresh spiritual insights. It may also signify someone who has the potential to radically transform your worldview or conditioned beliefs, or a time when you are driven to explore or question your own spiritual values and philosophies. This card may also encourage the pursuit of education or formal training. If you are searching for some greater purpose at this time or feel that you have deeper work to do, it may be helpful to think about what you would like to learn or change within yourself. What tools or resources can you connect with at this time? Whether it be a teacher, mentor, healer, therapist, spiritual guide, class, program, or community, now is the time to reach out.

QUESTIONS TO ASK

⚠ How do I celebrate my spiritual self?

⚠ What do I have yet to explore?

⚠ What brings me joy, peace, and happiness?

REVERSED

This might be an indication that you feel restricted in some way or are stuck in a situation you cannot get out of. It can also reflect a time in your life when you will need to follow your own path and go against the conventions that have been imposed upon you. A certain rebelliousness comes with the energy of the Hierophant when reversed—a need to revolt against the status quo and to break away from limitations or the norm. This card may also signify someone who is overly authoritative and domineering in your life that you may need to let go of. This is a wonderful time for you to stand on your own two feet with self-confidence and an awareness of your inner wisdom.

THE LOVERS

Keys: love • balance • marriage • proposals • celebration • choices • sexuality • unity • relationship • communication • friendship • completion • intimacy

THE LOVERS

The Lovers face one another in perfect love and trust—a sacred union of friendship and adoration. Shown here, they each hold an animal in their arms that they nurture and treasure: a representation of their individual life paths and responsibilities. Framed in the geometric form of the Vesica Piscis, they are the embodiments of two wholes—a synergistic expression of shared wisdom and respect. Above their heads floats the sacred Flower of Life, a lattice of the universal life force energy. Here, they reflect back to one another who they have been, who they are, and who they would ultimately like to become, together.

△ **Astrological:** Gemini, Mercury, Venus

△ **Gemstones:** Green Kyanite, Larimar, Rose Quartz

THE MESSAGE

An important relationship may be present in your life or near future: This could indicate a deep platonic friendship or romantic love. This card may describe the establishment of mutual respect and adoration between two individuals, as they honor and share personal beliefs and life values. It may also be the self-realization of that which is truly meaningful and spiritual through experiencing one another— mind, body, and spirit. Such strong and loving support gives you the safety and freedom to share your thoughts and feelings with this person. The choices you make, however, may greatly affect your future, so it is important to think them through on an individual level. Remember to mutually honor and celebrate your life paths; this will, in turn, bring strength into your relationships time and time again.

QUESTIONS TO ASK

⚠ What is my perception of true love?

⚠ Am I ready and open to receive love in abundance?

⚠ How am I honoring my own life path?

REVERSED

This card, when reversed, asks us to think about our notions of love and how these have been satisfied within our life. Have we been active in honoring the intentions of our hearts, and do we meet our partners and loved ones halfway? On a darker note, this may be an indication that there is some kind of imbalance in your life or in a relationship. Is something falling apart? Is there a shifting of values or beliefs? This card reversed may also denote an avoidance of certain responsibilities. It may be a good time to establish a sense of direction or priorities in order to make room for opportunities and growth.

THE CHARIOT

Keys: willpower • victory • movement • determination • confidence • transition • perseverance • ego

THE CHARIOT

The Chariot moves along freely as an expansive energy, racing forward without limitations or reins. This freedom of expression is embodied here in the form of a unicorn, a mystical creature that embraces its own unique journey. It knows there may be challenges ahead—uncharted paths, unknown strangers, and potential risks along the way—but rest is not an option. The power of the Chariot can be harnessed to fuel those sparks of inspiration or action that require our personal resolve and inner magic in order to reach our goals with confidence and ease.

⟁ **Astrological:** Cancer, Jupiter
⟁ **Gemstones:** Citrine, Peridot, Tiger's-eye

THE MESSAGE

The Chariot represents your inner strength, confidence, and steadfast determination in life. Typically identified as a card of victory and power, it signifies those moments when you have boundless spurts of energy and a sheer will to get things done! This is the adrenaline that keeps you motivated, the panic that helps you accomplish a huge goal in an extremely short amount of time, and the inspiration that drives your momentum. When you align with the power of the Chariot, anything is possible; however, it comes with a reminder that—yes—this might be a driving force but it's also an energy that cannot be maintained in the long run. Use it wisely, and appreciate its potency.

QUESTIONS TO ASK

⚠ What am I working toward?

⚠ Am I ready to move ahead in mind, body, and spirit?

⚠ How can I harness the energy of the Chariot in order to manifest my goals?

REVERSED

This may indicate a sense of helplessness, as if you have very little control over a particular situation (or of your life as a whole). It may denote a narrow focus, which might not be healthy in the long run. If you are feeling lost or stuck, think about how you are processing your thoughts and energy. Are you remaining confident in your choices, or are you feeling unsure of which direction to take? Take some time to meditate on what truly matters, and set your intentions clearly—in other words, go by your gut, your intuition, and what makes you feel good. Try navigating through what you can and cannot control at this time while being open to new changes or opportunities. Once you are able to grasp the reins of your own self-confidence, you will be able to assert a sense of direction again.

JUSTICE

Keys: equality • impartiality • contracts • truth • balance • fairness • wisdom • integrity • examination

Justice reflects the search for higher truth, integrity, and fairness. She stands upright, strong in her convictions, her feet rooted firmly on the ground. In her right hand, she wields a sword—a tool of steadfast precision and logic. At her left side rests an evenly balanced scale—a universal symbol for a transcendent moral code, the internal, intuitive compass that resides within us all. Justice asks us to put aside our emotions and attachments, allowing us to view the situation with impartiality, on a larger scale.

△ **Astrological:** Libra, Venus

△ **Gemstones:** Chrysolite, Emerald, Green Tourmaline

THE MESSAGE

This card may indicate a period of deep contemplation as you look to solve a problem or challenge. It is important to understand that the actions you take, the words you speak, and the thoughts you have will directly shape your reality. Justice is a card of energy transference; it describes the cause-and-effect balance of positive or negative thoughts and actions. How can you learn from experience? You will gain a loving wisdom and deeper spiritual knowledge once you are able to reflect on the choices you have made in the past. Be fair with yourself and others. It is important not to make assumptions and to remain as objective as you can.

QUESTIONS TO ASK

⚠ How can I reflect on my life and take positive steps from here?

⚠ How can I transform my view of this situation?

⚠ How have my thoughts directed my choices and actions in the past?

REVERSED

It could be that you are losing touch with a larger issue that may be affecting your life. This lesson may repeat itself until you become aware of what it is. It is important to understand that each experience is an opportunity for growth: You are on your own karmic path of learning and enlightenment. Try not to be biased in your perspectives, as a silver lining may yet present itself. How can you look beyond the stress or challenges of the situation in order to find the light that is readily available to you?

THE HERMIT
(SERENITY)

Keys: spiritual quest • meditation • introspection • consciousness • solitude • retreat • wisdom

The Hermit sits in restful solitude beside a quiet, still lake. Here, she experiences no external distractions, and the stars above her are crystal clear. In this moment, she holds her own space, aligning with her Higher Self and deeper intuitive strength. To get to this point, you may need to commit to going it alone. However, to reach a state of illumination, you don't need to be completely cut off from the outside world. Instead, the Hermit encourages us to seek our own inner sanctuaries, to detach from the fleeting interferences that are not healthy for us in the long run.

△ **Astrological:** Virgo
△ **Gemstones:** Amethyst, Celestite, Moonstone

THE MESSAGE

There is nothing wrong with seeking out your own space, as moments of solitude may offer new spiritual insights and revelations. The Hermit, or Serenity, describes a soul-searching journey in the pursuit of truth, purpose, and harmony. You may be waking up to a renewed spirituality that is illuminating your life in fresh and vibrant ways. The Hermit asks us to consider how we can strengthen or empower our own voice and not be swayed by another's influence or conditioning. While introspection is a helpful way to discern the truth, it does not mean we need to close ourselves off entirely. This card has both its benefits and downfalls: On the one hand, it helps us connect with who we are on a soul level, and on the other, it can indicate isolation or disconnection from others if we are not careful. Take a moment to reconnect with nature and explore the mysteries of the earth around you.

QUESTIONS TO ASK

⚠ What higher teachings are being presented to me at this time?

⚠ How can I connect with my true spiritual nature and Higher Self?

⚠ How can I surround myself with like-minded people?

REVERSED

If you are struggling to connect with your Higher Self or spiritual nature, you may need to set aside some time that is just for you. It could be that you will need to detach yourself from a group or from the presence of others for a short while in order to renew your sense of independence and clarity. If you find that you are, conversely, perhaps spending too much time in isolation, it might be a good time to reach out and seek connections with others. This can also indicate an opportunity to reestablish a sense of strength within your existing relationships.

THE WHEEL OF FORTUNE

Keys: cycles • transformation • transition • change • new beginnings • life lessons • karma • patterns

THE WHEEL OF FORTUNE

In this representation of the Wheel of Fortune, a young woman appears deep in thought. A heavy energy fills her mind; perhaps she is overthinking matters, but it feels as though she has zero control at the moment. She knows she isn't immune to the tides of change and that there are often forces that are beyond her grasp. Through these, the deeper life lessons emerge out of the darkness, and, because of this, she is able to put everything into perspective and have faith that things may eventually shift for the better. Tomorrow is a new day, and the world awaits with endless possibility.

⚠ **Astrological:** Jupiter
⚠ **Gemstones:** Smoky Quartz, Malachite, Black Tourmaline

THE MESSAGE

Just as the seasons change in an eternal cycle of energy, so does the path of your life. Understanding the Wheel of Fortune results in a state of acceptance of the highs and lows we face. With this comes a greater awareness of fate or potential opportunity, depending on how you look at it, encouraging us to identify the underlying patterns that repeatedly emerge over time. It indicates the habits we eventually learn to break and the karmic lessons that persist throughout lifetimes and experiences. Its greater message has to do with how we choose to react and respond to circumstance. Because of this, a great transformational energy moves through the Wheel of Fortune in that it pushes us to shift our views of the world and not take the precious moments for granted. Sometimes we are up; sometimes we are down. How can we take it all in stride?

QUESTIONS TO ASK

⚠ How can I learn from the choices I have made?

⚠ What patterns seem to be repeating in my life?

⚠ Is there a greater lesson being presented to me at this time?

REVERSED

You may feel as though you have had some bad luck due to a turn of events that has left you feeling rather helpless. There may be negative external forces influencing your situation. Think back: Have you made any choices that are contributing to the present challenge? How can you regain control of your perspective in order to move forward? Visualize yourself taking the necessary steps toward achieving your goals in as much detail as possible in your mind's eye.

STRENGTH

Keys: self-awareness • courage • self-mastery • confidence
• determination • skill • restraint

STRENGTH

In the space of a vast desert, a young woman stands with a great lion— a creature that embodies all that is wild and free, a representation of our innermost desires and passions. At its side, she seems unaffected by its presence, for in her grace and strength she has built a safe relationship with the lion. Both demonstrate a strong sense of mastery over their instincts, which is the deeper energy at the heart of this card. Within this meaning is the understanding that we are each animalistic in some way or another yet possess the strength to tame our wilder traits and give them healthy expressions and outlets.

⚠ **Astrological:** Leo
⚠ **Gemstones:** Bloodstone, Cinnabar, Hematite

THE MESSAGE

Your strength and courage will only increase as you believe in your innate ability to learn, heal, and evolve. This powerful card concerns the emergence of your Higher Self—one that is full of grace, love, and compassion. You are strong enough to navigate through any challenges and obstacles, a fact that emphasizes your ever-expanding state of consciousness. Understanding how strength comes mostly from within is directly related to the ways in which you harness your energy; this, in turn, will lead to spiritual growth as you are able to identify the vibrational qualities of your thoughts. Remember, it is important to treat others with compassion, love, and kindness, as strength also comes from being mindful of how we interact and communicate with the people around us.

QUESTIONS TO ASK

⚠ How am I acknowledging my inner strength and facing my fears?

⚠ What have I learned, after all that I have been through?

⚠ How can I shift my mindset in order to be empowered?

REVERSED

This could indicate a lack of self-determination or courage to move forward. Self-doubt may begin to creep into your thoughts, which can cause you to lose your self-confidence. It is important to remember the wisdom and courage you hold within. If you have relied on the reassurance or direction of others so far, now may be a good time to step out on your own and face your fears independently. You already have the skills and abilities you need to follow through with your plans. It is up to you to realize the root of your potential and to see how gifted and brilliant you truly are. Give yourself the benefit of the doubt.

THE HANGED MAN
(PERSPECTIVE)

Keys: crossroads • acceptance • epiphanies • patience
• surrender • sacrifice • introspection • meditation

PERSPECTIVE

A woman looks out into the distance: She is a mirrored image of herself—a parallel between two vantage points. Quietly, she reflects on her choices and surroundings. She is at a stage in her life when she knows change is inevitable and can feel it at the very core of her being. Depicted in traditional decks as a man hanged by his right foot, this card is the direct precursor to the Death card: a gateway into the inevitable metamorphosis that comes with letting go of something significant. Acts of surrender and release may lead to higher forms of knowledge and awareness. This represents the ultimate paradigm shift.

⚠ **Astrological:** Neptune
⚠ **Gemstones:** Azurite, Celestite, Sodalite

THE MESSAGE

Now might be a good time to pause, take a deep breath, and review your plans. If you're feeling stuck, don't make any hasty decisions just yet. If you sense that you are standing at a crossroads, take this time to fully absorb the directions or options that are being presented to you. Perhaps there is more than one solution being offered. It may be that you will need to let go of something or make some kind of sacrifice, which may initially leave you feeling vulnerable. This is a transitional phase during which you can recalibrate your beliefs, situation, or goals. This might also come as the result of life-altering moments that have the potential to transform your worldview, focus, or deeper priorities. Meditate on your personal hopes and dreams. When one door closes, another always opens.

QUESTIONS TO ASK

△ What are my options at this time?

△ Where do my true passions lie, and how am I honoring them?

△ How can I take a moment to pause and collect my thoughts before I make the next move?

REVERSED

This could be an indication that you have been making countless sacrifices without experiencing a proper payoff, which might temporarily delay the progress you had hoped for. Perhaps you are feeling stuck in a situation you cannot get out of. It is important to let go of any judgments or expectations you may have imposed on others or yourself. If you are feeling as though you are in a state of limbo, review your plans and intentions carefully. Are you taking the time to explore what makes you truly happy, or are you being pressured onto an uncomfortable path? Pause to mull things over, and surrender to your inner light.

DEATH
(TRANSFORMATION)

Keys: spiritual growth • relationship shifts • searching for deeper meaning • new beginnings • cycles of change • metamorphosis • transition

At a columned gateway, we see a figure passing through a threshold into an unknown space ahead. As she takes her next step into full awareness, she mentally and emotionally releases what no longer serves her. Above her in the distance floats a celestial light—a connection to the embrace of the universe, which provides her with all the lessons and experiences she needs. Just as the Wheel of Fortune heralds the tides of change, Death, or Transformation, encourages us to let go of certain energies, burdens, or unhealthy attachments, allowing us to envision a brighter future.

△ **Astrological:** Scorpio
△ **Gemstones:** Apophyllite, Moldavite, Rainbow Quartz

THE MESSAGE

Death, or Transformation, tends to show up when something is coming to an end and you must come to terms with how this will affect your life. At first, you might find it painful or even scary to let go of it, but, in the long run, this will create space and room for you to breathe and just be. This card may also reflect an entry point into an entirely new state of understanding or awareness, when major shifts begin to stir within you or in your life. When you hit rock bottom, end a relationship, decide to quit your job, or want a fresh start, this reevaluation of old patterns or beliefs may force you to eliminate the distractions or difficulties you have been experiencing thus far. Are you ready to take the next evolutionary step in your personal growth? Be open to new opportunities that present themselves, especially if they align with your heart.

QUESTIONS TO ASK

△ What do I need to release and let go of?

△ What has been holding me back?

△ Am I ready to look within in order to move ahead?

REVERSED

When reversed, Death, or Transformation, can be an indication that you are resisting some kind of inevitable change or are holding on to something that no longer serves you. You may also be close to an opportunity that you are not fully aware of. It may be helpful to face any past blockages or issues that are still putting pressure on you, in order to make room for positive changes. You are going to need to reach a sense of closure before moving forward, or this lesson may resurface in the future. Now might be a good time to look ahead with optimism and strength—you are on the right path.

TEMPERANCE

Keys: harmony • balance • renewal • adaptation
• moderation • healing • duality • spirit guide

Standing in a pool of water, a celestial being connects with the earthly realm below and the grace of the cosmos above. With her are two cups, representing the sub- and super-conscious minds, which she blends together effortlessly. This card prompts us to think about how we can moderate our thoughts for the greater good of our higher awareness and spiritual well-being. If we find balance, we can maintain a neutral approach in how we choose to view the world around us. As nothing is finite, Temperance reminds us of the universal harmony and synergy of all matter.

△ **Astrological:** Sagittarius
△ **Gemstones:** Amazonite, Blue Kyanite, Blue Lace Agate

THE MESSAGE

Temperance encourages us to be mindful of any decisions we make at this time. There may be a need for balance, moderation, or a reassessment of personal goals. In the grand scheme of things—and after everything you have been through—it is important to connect with the larger scope of your life. What gives you a sense of purpose and joy? Temperance reminds us to be patient, loving, and caring in order to manifest our hopes and dreams. This card may also be an indication that you should bide your time with any long-term goals and advance gracefully and methodically with your plans. Harmony comes with moderation in all things: mind, body, and spirit. Spiritual growth comes from learning life lessons through a myriad of experiences— both positive and negative.

QUESTIONS TO ASK

⚠ What is my greatest block at this time?

⚠ How will I ascend to my next spiritual stage of learning?

⚠ What deeper learning do I wish to explore at this time?

REVERSED

You may feel as though things are not moving forward, despite your efforts and desires. It is important to find a sense of balance at this time. What is missing? Are you obsessing over something that is taking over other areas of your life? You may need to ground yourself and meditate on the issues at hand. Perhaps you will have to let go of something or make some kind of sacrifice in order to create room for new opportunities. Take some time to look ahead and envision your future—there is much to look forward to!

THE DEVIL
(OPPRESSION)

Keys: ego • ignorance • dependency • temptation • debt • excess
• materialism • habitual worry • addiction • bondage

OPPRESSION

A veiled, ghostly figure floats above the ground, suspended between the earthly plane and spirit world. Here is a universal energy that has the potential to haunt each of us at some point. Typically depicted as one of the greatest antagonists of our time, the Devil, or Oppression, has been known to hide behind the destructive tendencies that we carry within ourselves. Whether in the form of addiction, our ego, a materialistic mindset, a negative ancestral pattern, or a self-inflicted dependency that is stunting our spirit, there is a certain willfulness in this sort of behavior that needs to be addressed.

△ **Astrological:** Capricorn
△ **Gemstones:** Black Tourmaline, Fire Opal, Obsidian, Onyx

THE MESSAGE

What is holding you back at this time? Perhaps you already know what it is, but you have not been able to name it out loud. It is time to acknowledge a state of entrapment that exists in your life. This could take the form of a negative relationship, an obsession, a fearful mindset, or some kind of addiction. The Devil may also indicate a lack of moderation or self-control, and the self-defeating patterns from which we must learn to release ourselves. Know that you are fully capable of breaking free from these habits in order to look back on this time with a sense of victory and relief. Something big needs to change. This card may also indicate that you may be too focused on the material things in life that are distracting you from acknowledging your spiritual self.

QUESTIONS TO ASK

⚠ How can I break free from the bonds that have been holding me back?

⚠ What will help me feel more at peace?

⚠ Is there something that I am obsessing over at this time?

REVERSED

It is important to bring your attention to any potential negativities in your life. Perhaps there are people, substances, or temptations that may not be good for you in the long run. Remaining detached and uninfluenced allows you to gain a stronger sense of self while disconnecting from the negative energies surrounding you, which is important for your spiritual growth and overall health. This is an opportune time for you to focus on your own well-being and personal development. A period of great change and transformation.

THE TOWER

Keys: loss of stability • abandoning old relationships • transformation • moving into the unknown • inevitable change • upheaval • liberation • new beginnings

The Tower stands as a great monument of change and transformation. Beneath its shadowed presence sits a quiet figure, lost within its impending energy. Lightning strikes the Tower, shaking loose the foundations of its structure. This chaotic force illuminates and exposes the wreckage that is unraveling around her. The gray clouds that hover above are indicative of nearing misfortune. The moon represents the shadows ahead, while the sun will have the power to break through the darkness once the dust has settled.

⚠ **Astrological:** Mars
⚠ **Gemstones:** Hematite, Prehnite, Serpentine

THE MESSAGE

The Tower indicates a period of complete or sudden change. You may experience a sense of insecurity or loss—as if your world has been flipped upside down. It can also denote situations in which the mind, body, and spirit are not working in harmony due to passive or unhealthy life choices. The Tower encourages you to examine old patterns or systems of belief, leading to fresh perspectives that are transformational and positive in the long term. This card may also indicate a breakthrough in consciousness, which allows you to realize that your personal growth lies in freeing yourself from the unnecessary burdens in your life. What is the greater lesson to be learned? Know that for every difficult situation we face, we are forced to grow from experience. Liberation comes from letting go and moving forward, and sometimes to do this we have to hit a low point. Without the dark, there is no light.

QUESTIONS TO ASK

⚠ Am I ready to face my own feelings throughout the stress and chaos?

⚠ What have I learned from this experience?

⚠ How will I cope with these energies?

REVERSED

When reversed, there is often a greater lesson to be learned in order to break free. You don't need this stress weighing on you any longer. It is time to build a new foundation for your life. This card denotes the intense, deeply meaningful lessons that are often revealed through devastations. As a result, your priorities may become crystal clear once everything else has been stripped away. What you have left are the exposed elements of your heart. Your pure intent. Your power and strength.

THE STAR

Keys: spiritual love · bright prospects · hope · inspiration
· new beginnings · success · creativity · healing

Seated at the edge of a sacred water bank, a woman rests in quiet solitude, peering out at the cosmic scene above. In this moment, she knows she can finally take a breath and relax, orienting her new position and role in the world. Within her heart, a glimmer of hope begins to illuminate her path. Basking in the energy of a great star overhead, she thinks about how far she has come and where she would like to go from here. The water surrounding her reflects an intuitive wisdom, while the earthly foothills connect her with a grounding strength to build the life she desires.

△ **Astrological:** Aquarius
△ **Gemstones:** Amethyst, Celestite, Spirit Quartz

THE MESSAGE

A beautiful omen to receive, the gentle magic of the Star connects with your inner voice of inspiration and light. When it speaks, your heart lifts and your spirit soars. This marks a time of renewal and fulfillment, when the serendipitous magic seems to continuously unfold around you. The Star also indicates a good balance of creativity, work, and soulful aspirations while pointing toward new pleasurable interludes and experiences ahead. After emerging from a phase of instability or turmoil, you are now ready to replenish your spiritual and emotional reserves. As you bask in this expansive energy, you connect with a universal source of illumination—a mirrored reflection of your own self sparkling in the sky above. Each made of stardust, we are the boundless particles of the greatest cosmic consciousness of all.

QUESTIONS TO ASK

△ Am I ready to celebrate and honor the light that surrounds me?

△ How can I take the next evolutionary step in my own spiritual growth?

△ What messages do my spirit guides have for me at this time?

REVERSED

When reversed, the Star may indicate insecurity, self-doubt, or a sense of pessimism that leaves you yearning for the truth. It is important that you identify what is holding you back at this time; this might point to unfulfilled dreams or a certain lack of confidence in your skills and abilities. Look out for new sparks of inspiration and ideas that begin to stir within you: These are significant signs. When you are ready to move forward, you will experience the transformation you need. Don't be afraid to ask for guidance.

THE MOON

Keys: disillusionment • intuition • dreams • fear • mystery • imagination • shadow work • receptivity • magic

Overhead, the Moon illuminates a celestial path. Beneath its light stands a woman. Her hands are outstretched to meet its glowing embrace. She is deeply in tune with its secrets, mysteries, and perpetual rhythm—its powerful push and pull, which harmonizes with the tides of her body. Over the years, it also has borne witness to her emotions—when she was bursting with tears, beaming with light, and moving through the darkest and brightest times in her life. She is aware that countless others have also looked to it for answers, contemplating and worshipping its luminous mystical power.

Astrological: Pisces

Gemstones: Kyanite, Labradorite, Moonstone

THE MESSAGE

The Moon is a card of sensitivities, dreams, imagination, and psychic powers. Typically described as a harbinger of disillusionment, it is not without its more positive aspects; it can indicate the powerful sparks of inspiration that feed invention, creativity, and intuitive discoveries. It represents an ancient, arcane magic that resides within us all. As it is a watery card, it also embodies the mysterious depths of our minds, which we tend to keep hidden from others, as well as the deeper insecurities that plague our emotions. Since the Moon addresses our shadow thoughts and feelings, it is helpful to acknowledge these as the balancing contrasts to your lighter or happier facets, without letting them take over your mind completely. These are significant parts of who you are, and they are not without value, so now may be a good time to work with your shadow and connect with the root of your feelings. The power of your mind is limitless.

QUESTIONS TO ASK

⚠ How can I work with the darker aspects of my thoughts and feelings in order to move forward?

⚠ How can I work with my Shadow Self?

⚠ How can I tune into my psychic abilities?

REVERSED

This card reversed can be indicative of deception, confusion, or turmoil. If you are experiencing some kind of fear, it may be a good time to address this head-on. Listening to your dreams, psychic visions, and intuition will provide you with a clearer direction. Don't hesitate to reach out or seek counsel from those you trust. Try to acknowledge the roots of any negative feelings or emotions. Continue to confront your fears, and your self-confidence will only increase.

THE SUN

Keys: relationships • warmth • pleasure • sincerity • good health • joy • accomplishment • success • abundance • Inner Child

The Sun fills the sky with a golden radiance as the energetic counterpart to its sister, the Moon. Together, their cosmic dance reflects the universal balance of light and dark energies. Both moving through unique cycles of activity, they each have different roles to play. The Sun illuminates our shadows while also bringing light to our dormant creative energies. It is ancient and wise, and it embodies a potent magic and infallible perfection. Without its light, our world would cease to exist. It connects with our heart—the sun of the body—and radiates its life force into the depths of our spirit.

△ **Astrological:** The Sun
△ **Gemstones:** Carnelian, Citrine, Orange Kyanite

THE MESSAGE

When the Sun shows up in a reading, it is time to acknowledge your blessings. Here is an expansive, love-filled radiance that marks a joyous, magnificent time in your life. Along with a renewed sense of abundance, you have reached a higher state of consciousness: This elevates your inner growth and connects you with the divine light of Source energy. The Sun also reflects your positive mindset and how you choose to interact with others. You are succeeding in new and vibrant ways and are able to pour all of your enthusiasm and vitality into your dreams. When you resonate this way, it is only natural that more light will shine down upon you and the ones you love. Bask in this healing, transformational energy; it has guided you this far.

QUESTIONS TO ASK

⚠ How can I maintain this positive mindset and approach to life?

⚠ Am I ready to rejoice and celebrate after all of my hard work?

⚠ Am I ready to acknowledge the light in myself and others?

REVERSED

This may indicate a sense of loneliness or difficulty. Although you may at times feel strong in your convictions, there are perhaps moments when you repress your voice or opinions. If you feel as though your direction has been clouded, know that this is merely a temporary setback. Things will definitely shift for the better if you become mindful of your thoughts, your strengths, and the love and light that surrounds you. Take some time to reconnect with the activities you enjoy and the skills you have, and align yourself with new and exciting opportunities. If need be, reach out for support or to someone you love: The Sun can show up in all kinds of places.

JUDGMENT
(AWAKENING)

Keys: epiphany • ascension • enlightenment • purpose • forgiveness • new beginnings • renewal • breakthrough

AWAKENING

Kneeling beneath a twinkling sky, a traveler stops to rest at a great mountainous divide. Here, her mind awakens—suddenly coming into awareness of who she truly is. From below, she is grounded to the earth, while above, the divinity of the cosmos imparts its wisdom to her. As she looks inward, she reflects on the moments of her life— the heartache, the missed opportunities, the emotional shifts, and the personal choices—knowing each has been willed for her own inner growth. As she surrenders to the universe, she begins to feel at peace with her story.

⚠ **Astrological:** Pluto
⚠ **Gemstones:** Apophyllite, Moldavite, Spirit Quartz

THE MESSAGE

Often shown as a scene of the Last Judgment, this card is about understanding your inner divine intelligence. Here, you may look back on the choices you have made and identify the lessons you have learned, with each step advancing you toward a higher awareness of who you are at a soul level. No more fears. No more doubts. No more self-judgment. This is a time of transformation: Through elevating your thoughts, speaking your truth, and connecting with the light that ignites your dreams, anything is possible. Divine wisdom comes from relinquishing the negative feelings you have been harboring toward others or yourself. Holding on to guilt, fear, or resentment cannot serve you and prevents you from connecting with your Higher Self. This is the entry point into an entirely new chapter. Where will you go from here?

QUESTIONS TO ASK

△ Do I need to forgive myself or someone else?

△ What am I resisting at this time?

△ Am I ready to take the next step in my own healing and transformation?

REVERSED

This may indicate a reluctance to face an inner truth, or that you are burdened in some way. Perhaps you have been procrastinating or are experiencing self-doubt. Are there feelings of guilt that are plaguing your mind? Try to imagine yourself living and experiencing your life goals through visualization or meditation. By practicing this each day, you may shift your field of reality. Your power is limitless, as are your paths and infinite potentials.

THE WORLD

(THE UNIVERSE)

Keys: ascension • new opportunities • clarity • completion
• success • triumph • spiritual growth • celebration

At the end of a long journey, a young woman sits in quiet meditation beneath a great pyramid. In this sacred space, she can finally take in what she has built and experienced. As she reflects, she knows she has grown and pushed herself to the brink of potential. Her priorities have shifted, and she is seeing the world through a new lens. Above her head floats the bright light of a Star Tetrahedron, the Merkaba Vehicle of Light—a symbol of balance, duality, and intuitive wisdom. This marks her transition from individual consciousness to unity with the collective abundance of the universe.

△ **Astrological:** Saturn

△ **Gemstones:** Indigo Kyanite, Lapis Lazuli, Moldavite

THE MESSAGE

Everything has come full circle as you enter a period of resolution and enlightenment. This is the culmination of all of your efforts and hard work, so it is time to acknowledge and celebrate all of your accomplishments. There is a synthesis of success, fulfillment, and triumph in your undertakings. You are rising to a new level of excitement and spiritual fulfillment, which gives you a better understanding of your place in the universe. In working through the trials and tribulations of life, you have learned to grow from experience. As a powerful cocreator of your story, you now understand how the choices you have made have affected your karmic path. A new stage of your journey begins.

QUESTIONS TO ASK

⚠ How will I ascend now to the next stage of my spiritual journey?

⚠ Am I able to recognize all of my accomplishments and celebrate my story?

⚠ How has my perspective changed from this new place of illumination?

REVERSED

This may be an indication that you are falling short of achieving your fullest potential. Perhaps there has been an avoidance of certain necessary steps. If you have been holding on to issues or pains from your past, it is time to face these with compassion and self-love. From here, you may be ready to release these bonds and reflect on what you have learned and achieved. How happy are you in your life? Your world can be whatever you make it.

THE
MINOR
ARCANA

✦

THE
WANDS

ACE OF WANDS

Keys: creation • beginning • adventure • soul purpose • energy
• vitality • birth • inheritance • new relationships

As the first card of this dynamic, fiery suit, we see an individual, ornate wand that is ready to be wielded to its full potential. How will it be used? To cast a spell? Or ignite a dream? This one is alive, and we can still see lush petals growing from its branch. However you wish to use this light is up to you. Remember, this is just the beginning. Pure magic awaits!

THE MESSAGE

A wonderful new beginning full of inspiration, vitality, and movement! This is a seed of invention that has the potential to grow into something great and highlights new breakthroughs in consciousness. From here, anything is possible. Perhaps you are on the verge of trying something new or expanding your ideas. If there is anything you have been planning on pursuing, now is the time to take action. You have the skills and talents you need in order to manifest your creativity in all of its power. If this is the initial stage of your venture, know that you are heading into a life-changing period that is deeply rooted in your inner truth. As a result, you will find the creative outlets you need. A time for action and self-expression.

QUESTIONS TO ASK

⚠ How can I use my creativity to manifest my dreams to their fullest potential?

⚠ Am I ready to follow this new spark of inspiration?

REVERSED

A delay in progress. There may be unrealistic goals or expectations at this time. It could be a good time to review your plans before making any big decisions. How can you harness your creativity and inventive sparks in order to come up with an alternative solution? Take a moment to focus on your hopes and dreams. What makes you blissfully happy in life? Where do you want to go from here?

TWO OF WANDS

Keys: direction • invention • facing fears • seeking wisdom
• individuality • choice • partnerships • determination

TWO OF WANDS

Following on from the inventive magic of the Ace, the Two of Wands highlights the confidence and vision we need to manifest our plans. Here, we see two wands suspended above the hands of a young woman. She is ready to work her magic, but she must remember that there are in fact two wands at her disposal: How will she divide her powers between them both? If she is able to focus and be mindful of the larger scope of the situation, her output may double in strength.

THE MESSAGE

This card comes as a powerful reminder that you are capable of anything you
wish to accomplish when you focus your mind toward a specific task or goal. You
have acknowledged all of your options and can now look ahead with purpose
and determination. This is also a card of power and choice; it may be that you will
need to decide how to divide your energy among certain projects, relationships, or
opportunities. Perhaps it is time to step outside your comfort zone and try something
new? Two is a divisive number and speaks of splitting energies while also highlighting
the power of balance, cooperation, and synergy. If One is great, then Two is even
better; however, you will need to be conscious of all the minutiae of your plan. If you
combine your energies, expect a most magnificent outcome or return!

QUESTIONS TO ASK

⚠ How can I combine my efforts in order to achieve the best results?
⚠ How am I balancing my energies at this time?

REVERSED

This can indicate a time when we are feeling stuck or lacking a sense of direction.
If you are overly ambitious or eager, you may need to plan more carefully in order
to move forward in a positive light. A change is necessary, but don't be forceful or
impatient. Finding balance will help you take the next step. It may be a matter of
waiting a bit longer until you have reached a comfortable level of success.

THREE OF WANDS

Keys: being visionary • expanding your horizons • listening to your intuition • looking upward and inward

THREE OF WANDS

Seated at the edge of a stargate, a woman looks out into another world, focusing her intent on the journey ahead. This card highlights the intuitive foresight that allows us to envision the path that lies before us. We can see it. We can dream it. We can almost touch it, only now we must take action. The Three of Wands asks us to consider whether we are ready to cross the threshold into a new space of creation.

THE MESSAGE

The Three of Wands marks a time in your life when you can look to the future with total clarity. This wisdom comes from having the determination to walk your own path and be true to your heart. You are gaining momentum in achieving your dreams and are aware of how your creative planning has been pivotal in helping you make big decisions. This card is not necessarily about taking risks; rather, it highlights those moments when you study the path ahead in order to know exactly what tools or resources will be essential to your journey, and there is a certain strength that comes with this preparedness. Along with the excitement of adventure that lies within this card, perhaps you have a wonderful system of support from friends or family members that builds up your enthusiasm. Don't forget to treasure and soak up this love and magic—there is nothing greater than mutual support. The Three of Wands also indicates a higher state of awareness. You know what it takes to get things done.

QUESTIONS TO ASK

⚠ Am I ready to embark on a new journey?

⚠ What do I truly envision for my future?

REVERSED

The misuse of personal power or energies. How can you recognize the tools that are readily available to you? It's time to acknowledge where your talents and skills truly lie. Do not be discouraged if your plans fail at first; if you find a sense of balance and organize yourself accordingly, you will be able to get back on track. Remember to focus on your own goals before giving in to the needs of others.

FOUR OF WANDS

Keys: prosperity • peace • completion • stability
• celebration • spontaneity • freedom

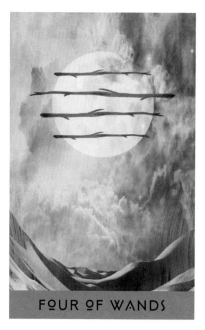

FOUR OF WANDS

The Four of Wands is a true reason to celebrate. Showing up as a blessing in your life, this card illuminates a period of harmonious change. The fruits of your labor, the silver linings—the sweet, sweet times! Here we see this card represented as a mystical scene: Four wands float above the face of the moon. Their structured power feeds and builds off one another to create a stable vision, yet they are free and yours for the taking.

THE MESSAGE

Success! You have reached a period of stability after all your hard work. This may also denote a time for repose or recovery once certain challenges or hardships have finally passed. There is much to look forward to, so give yourself permission to rest. With this outpouring of positive energy, it is also an ideal time to organize celebratory gatherings with family members and loved ones. An emergence of peace and happiness is on the horizon, and you understand the process and rewards of working hard toward your goals. You are able to nurture your loving relationships with others and bring wisdom and abundance into the lives of the people around you. After everything you have been through, your priorities are crystal clear.

QUESTIONS TO ASK

⚠ How can I connect with the people I love?
⚠ What do I truly prioritize and treasure in this life?

REVERSED

You may feel as though your energies have been wasted or a project or idea has been delayed. This may reflect an overall lack of harmony or inner peace at this time. It may also indicate a period of change or transition where you feel helpless or lack stability. An alternative approach to an issue may be needed. Take some time for yourself, and meditate on what it is you truly wish to achieve and build.

FIVE OF WANDS

Keys: competition • delays • unsatisfied desires • redirection of energies
• breaking away • independence

FIVE OF WANDS

Seated alone in a quiet space, a starlit figure pauses to think. She is filled with great ideas, bursting with light, yet feels as though certain obstacles have suddenly crossed her path. There is a sense of isolation that comes with this card in that it often highlights those moments when we don't know where we stand. In traditional representations, it can show youths fighting, and perhaps there are competitive energies exerting pressure on you, such as quarrels or frustration with others. This card encourages you to look within in order to find what you may be harboring or holding on to.

THE MESSAGE

The Five of Wands tends to show up when some kind of struggle is occurring in your life, whether you feel you must stick up for yourself or when there are surrounding ideas or values that clash with your own. This situation has come to a boiling point, and something's gotta give! This could also signify challenges within yourself that you are having to work through. At some point or other, these will make themselves known, whether through your behavior or stress levels. How can you focus your mind at this time? It could be that you will find yourself competing with someone who is equally ambitious. If you feel as though you have stumbled, know that you have the absolute strength to pick yourself up again. Now more than ever, it is important to honor your heart and make your priorities clear. This card is not about teamwork but personal goals and ambitions.

QUESTIONS TO ASK

⚠ Am I ready to work through this temporary obstacle?
⚠ How can I focus my mind in order to shift the energy of this situation?

REVERSED

This may indicate a reluctance to express inner thoughts or feelings, as there may be conflicting energies or difficulties in making meaningful connections with others. If you have experienced stress as a result of passive-aggressive or competitive behavior from someone around you, take some time to disconnect from these lower vibrational energies. It could be that you simply need to regain a sense of peace and independence in order to feel good again.

SIX OF WANDS

Keys: accomplishment · diplomacy · conquest · good fortune
· cooperation · popularity · success · pride

Making her own magic, a sorceress sits here at the edge of a great mountain. She has harnessed and mastered her work and is now receiving the reward she so richly deserves. She is her greatest ally, her own best source of support. In this moment, she feels greatly accomplished and absorbed in the center of her success.

THE MESSAGE

The arrival of positive news! You are victorious and should be proud of your brilliant accomplishments. Your enthusiasm has paid off threefold as you realize your limitless potential. There is nothing you cannot achieve, and others also recognize this strength in you. Creativity begins in connecting with your Higher Self: You have learned to harness this and are an inspiration to those around you. This card represents the harmonious state that comes from reaching a healthy and comfortable balance in all areas of your life—mind, body, and spirit. Yet, although this may be a great time to celebrate, try not to forget how you got to this point. The Six of Wands is indeed a positive message, but it can indicate excessive feelings of pride fueled by the ego if rewards are not accepted with gratitude as the blessings they are.

QUESTIONS TO ASK

⚠ How can I remain humble and grateful at this time?

⚠ How can I celebrate all that I have worked for and achieved?

REVERSED

The existence of setbacks or delays in your plans. It is important to review your goals and direct your energy into your true life priorities. Constructive planning is needed in order to move forward victoriously. Overoptimism may be jeopardizing your efforts. Take some time to nurture your talents in order to manifest your dreams.

SEVEN OF WANDS

Keys: gain • competition • creative abilities • success within reach
• protection • defiance

Looking out into the great beyond, a woman sits calmly next to a tiger. This creature is strong and grounded. It knows when to make the next move, and here she aligns with its energy, preparing herself for the plan ahead. Sometimes depicted as a yeoman fighting for his land, there is a certain warrior energy that comes with the Seven of Wands, marking a time when you must be courageous and headstrong.

THE MESSAGE

The Seven of Wands serves as a positive reminder that your life is heading in the right direction. You have worked hard and know what you want, so don't be discouraged by any minor setbacks that may show up along the way. This could also indicate a time when the momentum of your success will require your personal resolve and courage when dealing with other people, so it is important to stay strong and assert yourself. Do not be afraid to speak your truth. This is a very dynamic and energetic time in your life, so remember to celebrate all of your accomplishments as you move forward. Any new projects or ideas will require your full attention, planning, and innate skills. You know what you need to do.

QUESTIONS TO ASK

⚠ How can I pick and choose my battles?

⚠ From where do I draw my inner strength?

REVERSED

When reversed, the Seven of Wands may indicate a sense of being overwhelmed, judged, or criticized by others. If you feel you have not been able to speak your truth or express yourself freely, it is important that you stand your ground and be strong in your convictions. How are you focusing your energies into what makes you happy? You will need to be clear in your intentions, or else you may find yourself stuck in a state of limbo or indifference.

EIGHT OF WANDS

Keys: adventure • change • newfound success • movement
• collaboration • successful timing • news

EIGHT OF WANDS

At the brink of dusk, a priestess begins to work her magic. Her spark of inspiration has been conjured from an intuitive vision: She is a creative force and knows that proper planning will be needed to manifest this thought. There is a strong feeling of movement in this card; at this point, the initial stages are being visualized, but the final outcome is not yet clear. Regardless of which, swift action will be paramount to the unfolding of this story. Now is not the time to delay efforts!

THE MESSAGE

The Eight of Wands is a card of swift action, transition, and positive news. Here is a creative force that requires your personal resolve and attention, perhaps with regard to new opportunities that are coming your way. This is the kind of energy that lights a fire beneath you, forcing you to get up and make things happen! If life has been feeling overwhelming, know that a positive change is still very possible—you may just need to think about how you are dividing your efforts. Now is the time to take action and set your intentions. Once you focus on a specific task or goal, there is nothing you cannot accomplish. This is the self-direction, determination, and confidence that comes from clarity, vision, and drive. The Eight of Wands may also highlight positive success through group strength and cooperation. A time to be decisive and courageous.

QUESTIONS TO ASK

⚠ What can I do to put things in motion?

⚠ How can I balance all that I am working toward?

REVERSED

Your situation may feel unstable, unresolved, or as though matters have been delayed. Are you feeling indecisive about a choice that needs to be made? There could be a loss of opportunity if you cannot focus your energy authentically. You may need to find a creative alternative to a situation or give yourself a bit more time. Try taking smaller (and more comfortable) steps instead of forceful leaps and bounds.

NINE OF WANDS

Keys: perseverance • courage • strength • stability • stamina
• performance • preparedness • awareness

In this image we see the form of a glowing Crown Chakra—a symbol for our universal connection to the Source of our higher awareness. It encourages us to look inward, beyond the limitations of the ego, enabling us to explore our personal development and inner growth. This journey is ours, and we are reaching new heights of wisdom; now is the time to look ahead with optimism and strength. Framing this chakra are the forms of nine wands, individual representations of our human experiences or emotions.

THE MESSAGE

Just as you see light at the end of the tunnel, a minor setback may suddenly get in the way. This card asks you to step into your resilience—you are almost there, so now is not the time to give up! Your hard work and efforts are close to a state of completion, and you have the inner strength, wisdom, and perseverance to keep up your momentum. Know that you are incredibly close, so it is important not to lose touch with your goals, even if the path seems difficult to navigate. Believe in yourself and your innate ability to achieve success. After this last challenge you will know what you are fully capable of. On another note, this card may indicate that you are beginning to see where you have fallen short in life and how your habits, actions, words, or thoughts may have hindered your advancement. This can give you a fresh understanding of how to shift things for the better from now on.

QUESTIONS TO ASK

⚠ Where do my greatest priorities lie?
⚠ How can I reconnect with my heart center?

REVERSED

This card can show up reversed during those moments in life when things feel outright overwhelming due to responsibilities or limitations. These pressures may create boundaries surrounding your sense of freedom and self-expression, manifesting in those lower vibrational emotions (like resentment, jealousy, or fear) that tend to hold us back. If you are subconsciously feeling tormented about something, this in turn may lead to a sense of your being judged or criticized by others. Now may be a good time to work on your spiritual health—mind, body, and spirit. Give yourself some time.

TEN OF WANDS

Keys: external forces • balance • time management • overstimulation • grounding • burden • being overwhelmed

In this card, we see a woman being divided into two different roles. She finds herself off-balance, being pulled in countless directions, a heavy weight overshadowing her life. This comes as a result of her not being able to focus her energy into one clear path. Over time, this burden will weaken her spirit if she is not able to break free.

THE MESSAGE

After all you have achieved, you may feel overburdened by responsibilities, finding yourself overworked or somehow out of kilter. The Ten of Wands may also indicate an emotional attachment or experience that you are still harboring that is depleting your energy and distracting you from the larger scope of your life. Your initial aspirations or dreams may seem faded from your present situation if you are losing your creative momentum. Now might be a good time to accept help from others and prioritize what is truly necessary. How are you gaining wisdom from your actions? What can you remove or cut out in order to reduce some of the pressure on yourself?

QUESTIONS TO ASK

⚠ What can I release or let go of at this time?

⚠ How can I shift the energy of this burden?

REVERSED

You may be experiencing oppressive responsibilities or are unable to remove yourself from a stressful situation. This might be an opportune time for you to focus on your dreams and personal aspirations in order to remove any limitations and pressures that have been present in your life. It is time to release and purge the energies that are holding you back. Is there someone you can reach out to? How would you like to focus your energy first and foremost?

PAGE OF WANDS

Keys: confidence • courage • innocence • rebelliousness
• petulance • messenger • invention

PAGE OF WANDS

A budding dream has set this journey in motion. The Page of Wands is about to embark on a vision quest of her own making. Her adventurous mindset allows her to imagine the bright opportunities that are surely waiting for her. She is wild and free, ready to step over the threshold: The future is unwritten and hers for the taking.

THE MESSAGE

There may be new events and opportunities ahead. Be sure to move forward with clear intentions, always remembering the root of your confidence. The fruition of creativity and ideas. New adventures just beyond the horizon.

PEOPLE

The Page of Wands is an outgoing, enthusiastic individual who is energetic and risk taking. Their innocence gives them a certain fresh outlook, which may be a blessing in disguise. They have not yet been influenced by the stress of the world, which allows them to savor life's simple pleasures. But because of this, certain lessons may take longer to sink in. This generally has to do with their penchant for adventure, which defines their passage into adulthood. Each new day is an opportunity for experience, and they don't have time to slow down and pause. Despite this energy, this person is a positive omen and celebrates that spark of adventure we should all try to hold on to. Don't forget to savor it when it comes.

QUESTIONS TO ASK

⚠ What am I envisioning for my future?

⚠ How can I connect with new experiences and opportunities?

REVERSED

A lack of ambition or direction. Plans or ventures have yet to come to fruition, as a state of balance may be needed. This position may also have to do with the unreliability or detachment of another. A need to face truths and fears and to acknowledge pressures or constraints. The purging of negative attachments in order to start afresh.

KNIGHT OF WANDS

Keys: self-assured • fearless • confident • restless • daring
• impatient • quest • adventure

KNIGHT OF WANDS

The Knight of Wands stands ready for adventure at the edge of a forest. At one with the elements, he knows how to harness and channel their power to his greatest advantage. Through his self-assurance and intellectual prowess, he is confident that he has the foresight to set things in motion. There is a charm about him: He knows how to communicate successfully with others, which in the long run only helps his quest when aid is needed.

THE MESSAGE

You are making things happen! After everything you have worked toward and experienced, your personal goals and ambitions have become crystal clear. Make sure to plan accordingly, or else you might feel rushed when it comes to getting things done.

PEOPLE

The Knight of Wands is ready for anything and will likely attract accelerated, boundless energy into your life. He is smart and funny, and he has no problem connecting with people and can make anyone feel special in the moment. When it comes to his personality, whether he is charming or leaving you in the dust with reckless abandon, his emotional spectrum inclines toward extremes. When the Knight of Wands is directed by love, however, he is able to balance his emotions, actions, and thoughts in order to take control of his life. The Knight of Wands is also very determined when it comes to getting things done; he has the vision and drive to reach his goals but can sometimes be too hasty or impulsive.

QUESTIONS TO ASK

⚠ How can I take the next step in my spiritual learning?
⚠ What am I taking for granted at this time?

REVERSED

Feeling stuck or frustrated due to external pressures. There may be a lack of inner strength or a crisis of confidence. A need to understand how actions and thoughts may affect other people. Foolish risk taking or impulsivity without thinking of the consequences along the way.

QUEEN OF WANDS

Keys: optimistic • authoritative • spiritual • practical • independent • charismatic • attractive • visionary

QUEEN OF WANDS

Standing at the edge of her domain, the Queen of Wands is a magnetic force who knows her place in the collective consciousness. There is a divine fire within her personality, as she is strong and assertive yet knows the importance of kindness and generosity. The Queen of Wands walks her own path, charting a course that aligns with her heart and spiritual nature. Here at her side stands her familiar—a spirit animal who is fierce, protective, and loving.

THE MESSAGE

It is important to acknowledge your limitless potential! You are capable of accomplishing anything you wish if you put your mind to the task. Maintaining a positive mindset attracts an abundance of light into your life—the first step toward manifesting your dreams.

PEOPLE

The Queen of Wands is an extremely outgoing, generous person who is both strong-willed and fierce. She is fully aware of how her unwavering kindness and intelligence have shaped her beauty over the years, and, through her own set of standards, she celebrates and embodies her sexuality. This person does not need the assurance or validation of anyone else and lives her life freely without apology. She is highly protective and involved in the lives of her friends and family. She is also able to adapt well in almost any social environment, making all who surround her feel warm and welcome. The Queen of Wands may also become fiery, stubborn, and uncompromising when things don't go her way. Due to her strong temperament, there may be a tendency for extroverted communication and for placing draining emotional demands on those closest to her.

QUESTIONS TO ASK

⚠ How can I nurture my Divine Feminine nature?

⚠ How can I celebrate and rejoice with the people I love?

REVERSED

Impatience, aggression, or insensitivity. A very ambitious, stubborn mindset. Someone dependent on others yet indifferent to outside opinions. It may also indicate a lack of self-confidence in communicating and can relate to fearing the views of others who can see through the negativity.

KING OF WANDS

Keys: capable · enthusiastic · motivational · entrepreneurial
· influential · charismatic · manipulative

The King of Wands stands beneath the great expanse of his earthly and celestial domain. He is bold and charismatic and knows how to move mountains. He has been there, done that, yet keeps his high standards to himself, quietly viewing the world around him from a place of indifference and spiritual resolve. If you need his help, he is more than willing to offer his two cents. His visionary philosophy has taken him places in life, and he needs no validation or introduction. His reputation speaks for itself.

THE MESSAGE

You are a strong leader and attract like-minded people to you, just as others look to you for guidance. Your vitality and enthusiasm inspire the world, as you are able to come up with creative and complex ideas with confidence and ease. If there are any opportunities presenting themselves to you at the moment, now is the time to seize them.

PEOPLE

The King of Wands is a confident and sociable person. Typically viewed as a leader, he possesses his own pronounced power, radiating success through every fiber of his being. He knows he's smart, good-looking, and stylish, but he keeps this to himself. And nowhere is his passion more clear than in his work, where he stands out amid the crowd. Being perceptive of the skills and abilities of others, he is also highly supportive and compassionate, offering unconditional encouragement to those who seek his wisdom. Only truly inspired and entertained when surrounded by people of equal measure, the King of Wands lives by a code of personal ambition that, at times, seems almost superhuman. How does he do it all without breaking a sweat?

QUESTIONS TO ASK

⚠ How am I connecting with the people around me?

⚠ Am I making time for a deeper spiritual practice in my life?

REVERSED

A fiery personality that can sometimes appear harsh or insensitive to others. This card reversed might relate to an energy that is overbearing, controlling, or authoritative. It may also denote personal standards or expectations that are exerting pressure on you.

THE
CUPS

ACE OF CUPS

Keys: motherhood • marriage • intimacy • good health • friendship
• romantic love • psychic growth

As the first card of this dreamy, intuitive suit, we see an individual cup resting in a watery scene—a replenishing backdrop for the happiness that is being drawn upon. In this vessel, we see three precious crystals, all positive omens of fulfillment—and yours for the taking. As one of the most celebratory cards of the Tarot, the Ace of Cups marks a time of fresh beginnings and spiritual love.

THE MESSAGE

The Ace of Cups marks a time of new beginnings and blissful relationships that leave you feeling energized and giddy! This could point to new romance or deeply rooted connections with others. It is a powerful force that concerns the emergence of Universal Love and the cosmic ties you share with soul families and friends. Your psychic awareness might also be heightened at this time, allowing you to see beyond the veil of the 3-D world. This Ace also relates to the strength of your identity, self-esteem, and personal convictions; it is a wisdom that leads to new spiritual insights and deeper illumination. A wonderful period to explore original avenues of self-expression and creativity, which will raise your vibration to a whole new level!

QUESTIONS TO ASK

△ Am I ready to connect with the love around me?

△ How can I learn to love myself more?

REVERSED

You may be experiencing a state of sadness, loneliness, or disappointment. It could be time to look at why these feelings are surfacing—is there someone you need to forgive or a memory you may want to process? It is important to listen to your intuition and forge new habits of self-care and positive visualization. What can you do for yourself in order to shift the energy of your situation? How can you bring new opportunities into your life? Now is a time to be gentle with your heart.

TWO OF CUPS

Keys: cooperation • engagement • passion • resolution • union • lust • reconciliation • self-love

TWO OF CUPS

Very much like the Lovers card, the Two of Cups marks a time when loving connections are made. In this particular image, we see a young woman floating in a pool of water. She is weightless, free, and enjoying the sensation of being physically supported. There is a harmonious balance in this space: Above her, a rainbow glows between two cups, indicating a potential bond with a future lover. For now, she is learning to love herself, appreciating who she is and how far she has come. When love arrives, she will recognize its truth.

THE MESSAGE

This is a card of partnerships, love, and deep friendships. It represents a strong mutual connection and an affinity for positive, loving respect. You have released any blockages that have been exerting pressure on you, and now you can breathe and relax. The Two of Cups is also a card of new beginnings and budding romance. It may indicate an early phase when two people first meet, lost in a wave of infatuation. It is a dreamlike state where long-term goals may not be so clear. On another note, the Two of Cups can represent the emergence and importance of self-love. It is the understanding that in order to be happy in a relationship, you must first and foremost meet yourself halfway. This card may also identify the need for compromise or for a choice to be made in order to arrive at a comfortable solution between two people or opposing forces.

QUESTIONS TO ASK

⚠ What is my true perception of love?

⚠ How can I learn to appreciate and love my own self first?

REVERSED

When reversed, the Two of Cups can point to emotional blockages either within yourself or a relationship. Due to past traumas or experiences, there may be unresolved issues that are preventing positive outcomes or connections. A period of adjustment. It could be that there is some kind of dishonesty occurring. Things have shifted. The honeymoon phase is ending. Gossip. Unsatisfactory love. A misunderstanding. Time to speak your truth.

THREE OF CUPS

Keys: abundance • healing • solace • family • birth
• study • community • friendship • celebration

THREE OF CUPS

At the edge of a great mountain, a pyramid stands beneath the light of the moon. Near its cliffs flows an endless source of water, pouring life into the world below. Here we see three cups resting, waiting to be filled. There is an adventurous energy with this card—one that forecasts new celebrations and loving relationships. Once you reach the entrance of the pyramid, new insights and experiences are sure to unfold.

THE MESSAGE

The Three of Cups indicates a time of harmonious gatherings, creative energy, and the formation of lifelong memories. It can foretell an emergence of spiritual and psychic growth as you learn to raise your vibration to entirely new levels. This is an exciting time, so why not be with the ones you love? In surrounding yourself with your soul family—whether they are relatives or lifelong partners and friends—expect to create blissful memories together. If you have been overexerting yourself in some way, now may be an opportune time to relax and take a break. Give yourself permission to explore your own interests: Take a load off and put your feet up after you've had time to dance and celebrate! What future adventures lie just beyond the horizon?

QUESTIONS TO ASK

⚠ How can I make time for friends and loved ones?

⚠ Am I ready to take a break from my day-to-day life and relax in a harmonious space with others?

REVERSED

Setbacks or delays. Family quarrels or disputes. A state of unhappiness or instability. It may be time to have some important conversations with loved ones. If there are any issues from your past that are now resurfacing, take a moment to explore the depth of their implications. This allows you room for fresh perspectives and to perhaps even establish a sense of closure.

FOUR OF CUPS

Keys: disappointment • apathy • boredom • contemplation
• stress • doubt • introspection

FOUR OF CUPS

Slipping into a saddened state, a young woman sits here in quiet absorption. There is a moodiness to her. She can't find the words to articulate her feelings, and she takes no consolation or advice from others. Not even her darling cat can make her feel better at the moment. As she retreats into her loneliness, her thoughts become more intense, and her imagination gets the better of her.

THE MESSAGE

This card speaks of the tormented emotional states that can impair our grasp on reality. When depression, self-pity, or sadness sink in, and we retreat into our own world, our sensations and feelings can be overpowering and illusory. We may feel lost or hopeless or even outright bored, which may be an indication that we should consider our feelings head-on and examine our behavioral patterns or deeper motivations. Is there something you are suppressing or holding on to? Are there issues from your past that are weighing on your conscience? If you are fearful or indifferent about making a change, you might continue to dwell in limbo. This card also may suggest there is something you are overlooking; perhaps a solution is closer than you think. You have a system of love and support in your life: How can you connect with this? Are you alienating those around you who don't seem to get your point of view? Take a moment to meditate on the aspects of your life that you are truly grateful for.

QUESTIONS TO ASK

⚠ How can I work with my shadow thoughts in order to illuminate the root of my anguish?

⚠ How can I connect with my heart and break out of this stagnant pattern or routine?

REVERSED

You are close to breaking free from a state of stagnation or boredom. It is time to escape the routines or habitual patterns that have kept you trapped. If there are opportunities or new adventures calling you at this time, take a moment to consider them; they may very well be your ticket out. Now is the time to make positive changes in your life and to take action. Be open with your heart and feelings. An opportune time to focus on new projects and life goals.

FIVE OF CUPS

Keys: regret • obsession • self-pity • a need for forgiveness
• adjustment • loss • disappointment

FIVE OF CUPS

One of the more melancholy cards of the Tarot, the Five of Cups often points to moments of loss and disappointment. Here, we see five cups, each representing potential abundance, but one cup is sadly overturned, marking a loss that prevents us from celebrating the four that remain standing and full.

THE MESSAGE

The Five of Cups reflects the deep energies of change that emerge through instability or loss and may indicate a time of grief or stress as you struggle to see a way forward. Perhaps you are unable to identify the potential opportunities or support systems that surround you at this time, which in turn may trigger negativity as you lose sight of the positive blessings in your life. This may also have to do with unresolved issues from your past that might be affecting your emotional or spiritual health. This card can also highlight those moments in life when you find yourself being emotionally challenged to the max or when an inner survival mode kicks in. Know that a positive resolution is still highly possible, but it will depend on how you focus your energy and thoughts. Try not to resist the inevitable changes, or else you might find yourself repeating the same lesson again. This is a time of transformation and regeneration. Like the Death card, the Five of Cups asks us to consider how we can move forward after releasing unnecessary burdens.

QUESTIONS TO ASK

⚠ What is holding me back at this time?

⚠ Are there any painful issues from my past that need resolving?

REVERSED

This is a period of improvement and transformation. You can look back on the choices you have made and reflect on the outcomes and experiences you have gained. This is a card of new beginnings: You are ready to take the next steps in order to move forward with confidence and strength. If you are holding on to any suppressed feelings or pains, now may be the time to acknowledge these with self-love and compassion.

SIX OF CUPS

Keys: karmic connections • love • Inner Child • reconnection
• Akashic Records • ancestral patterns • innocence

Looking out into the distance, a young woman takes in the scene before her. It is the shadow of her childhood home, a place that once existed as a familiar presence in her life. Here, she sits and recalls the moments of her past, connecting with the fond, nostalgic memories of her heart.

THE MESSAGE

The Six of Cups shows up during those quiet moments of nostalgia that tend to take us back in time—sometimes these can be so intoxicating that triggered emotions rise to the surface, whether through reflecting on the incredible moments of our childhood or the underlying pains and traumas we experienced. These types of feelings can show up when we hear a certain song, smell a certain food, or pass an old house we once knew, and they embody the vivid fragments and chapters of our past. This card invites us to reflect on these memories and to seek out their greater implications and underlying energies. Is there a reason why we are holding on to these emotions or longings? As we are living records of every thought and feeling we have experienced, it is important to remember the Inner Child who still exists within you. Now may be a good time to plan out a recreational, social, or peaceful interlude. The Six of Cups may also reflect a period of relaxation and success after finally emerging from a stressful situation and highlights the self-confidence that comes from speaking your truth.

QUESTIONS TO ASK

⚠ How can I reconnect with my loved ones and soul family?

⚠ What memories do I tend to cling on to from my past?

REVERSED

A need to let go of past traumas or issues. It is important to recognize the gift of each and every moment in order to live fully in the present. Anticipating the future and reliving the past may detach you from the joy of living in the now. How can you build a new foundation of strength and support in your life?

SEVEN OF CUPS

Keys: wishful thinking • daydreaming • temptations
• choices • disillusionment • being overwhelmed

SEVEN OF CUPS

After a long stroll in the desert, we suddenly stumble upon an incredible vision! Here are seven glorious cups, each filled with sparkling crystals, which represent potential outcomes, dreams, and options to choose from. Is this an illusion? Which cup should we take? Or can we carry them all with us for the duration of our journey?

THE MESSAGE

The Seven of Cups marks a time in our life when we may feel overwhelmed with options and consequently cannot make a clear decision. This card might also indicate that we have unrealistic or illusory notions concerning what we can and cannot do. This feeds an unstable disconnect from reality—a dreamy sort of mindset that pushes us to indulge in certain things that aren't necessarily healthy or productive in the long term. In the end, we are faced with the consequences of our short-lived spurts of irresponsibility and grand illusions. The Seven of Cups is also a card of choices and temptations, dreams and desires. Perhaps we are subconsciously disconnecting from the truth because we do not want to face it. This card can also indicate delusions or fantasies about love and relationships. If you feel distracted by options, focus on the opportunities that align best with your long-term goals. Take some time to mull over your choices and envision what you really want. While these may be confusing times, the truth lies within your heart, so check in with yourself in order to see what you are truly feeling. Start from there and think about what you need to support yourself throughout this situation. Overcome your fears, and make a loving commitment to yourself.

QUESTIONS TO ASK

⚠ How am I going to share my talents and skills with the world?

⚠ What small steps can I take toward my goals?

REVERSED

Your thoughts or views may be unrealistic if you are projecting your fantasies into your life or onto others. An indifference or reluctance to acknowledge what truly makes you happy. Take some time to meditate on the positive steps you need to take in order to manifest what you truly want. Learn to differentiate between what you are unsure of and your deepest heart's desire.

EIGHT OF CUPS

Keys: moving on • abandonment • sacrifice
• growth • equanimity

At the edge of a great expanse, a young woman looks out into the distance. There is a deep sense of longing for a new world or way of life. Although she knows change may be inevitable and even healing in the long run, she is having difficulty letting go of that which no longer serves her higher calling. A deep reluctance comes with the energy of this card, although it does anticipate a time of transition and release.

THE MESSAGE

Sometimes depicting a traveler, the Eight of Cups represents a soul-searching journey during which you eventually feel the need to leave something behind. This could be triggered from a place of inner restlessness or unhappiness and marks a time of transition, deliverance, or coming to terms with certain burdens in your life. Know that letting go is often necessary for change; this could mean facing or healing painful memories, past relationships, or issues that are still affecting you. This release may foster an emotional strength that helps you navigate forward or deal with the stress or baggage of others. After shedding the unnecessary pressures in your life, you may find yourself seeking a more spiritual path.

QUESTIONS TO ASK

⚠ Am I ready to let go of what no longer serves me?

⚠ What has been holding me back from advancing my own spiritual growth?

⚠ Is there a direction that I would like to take from here on?

REVERSED

Do you need to process or let go of certain unresolved issues? If you are having difficulty making a decision, think about what you want your life to look like. What do you need to change in order to move forward with clarity and direction? It is important to face your fears and give yourself the benefit of the doubt.

NINE OF CUPS

Keys: romantic fulfillment • advancement • goodwill
• dreams • kindness • healing • abundance

NINE OF CUPS

Against a dreamy, watery backdrop, a woman stands beneath the promise of nine bountiful cups, each representing an energetic force of fulfillment and positive reward. She has reached a state of happiness and knows that luck is on her side. She soaks up this magic and feels gratitude for this healing phase of her life.

THE MESSAGE

One of the most joyful and harmonious cards of the Tarot, the Nine of Cups indicates a time of satisfaction and peace on the horizon! Often described as the "wish card," it highlights the fulfilled desires, happiness, and positive energies that surround you at this time. This leaves you with a sense of stability and strength but also comes with a slight caution; this blessing may not be permanent, so relish its magic while you can and accept it with gratitude. This card also asks us to consider the responsibilities and aftereffects that might ensue from positive events. When placed with other cards, the Nine of Cups can act as an enhancement of their energies. For example, when with Pentacles (or Crystals), it may be a strong indication of financial strength or material wealth coming your way. Look to the surrounding cards for its underlying message. Now, at last, is the time to enjoy life's well-deserved pleasures and luxuries. Your instincts are on high: Trust them.

QUESTIONS TO ASK

⚠ Am I ready to receive this gift with gratitude?

⚠ How am I celebrating my achievements?

REVERSED

When reversed, the Nine of Cups can describe unsatisfied desires, greed, or disillusionment. It's easy to forget that life can flip at any point, so this card encourages you to celebrate the good times as they come. It could also be that you already have everything you need, but something else is missing. Beyond physical wealth and stability, there might be an emotional lack in your life. How can you connect with your real desires without being overly attached to preconceived notions of happiness?

TEN OF CUPS

Keys: trust • romance • fulfillment • harmony • spiritual growth
• friendship • family values • cosmic ties

TEN OF CUPS

Standing together, here a coven of witches work their magic beneath the light of a dark moon. There is an unspoken bond between all three—an existing love that connects them throughout many lifetimes. They celebrate and rejoice deep into the night, taking comfort in the family and relationship they have built.

THE MESSAGE

The Ten of Cups is a magical, loving omen to receive. It signifies great happiness in all areas of family relationships, friendship, and love, and it asks you to make the most of what life has to offer. When this key shows up, things don't get much better than this. It represents an idyllic understanding of mutual respect, honor, and the cosmic bonds that connect you with others throughout lifetimes, as well as the spiritual foresight to walk your own path with honesty and integrity. When this card's greater implications are taken into consideration, you can let go of any worldly distractions and attachments that feed off of materialism, greed, and the ego. When you align with its energy, the silver linings are always visible. The glass is more than half full (it overflows!). A potent time of happiness and abundance is on the horizon!

QUESTIONS TO ASK

△ Am I ready to bask in this positive energy with the people I love?

△ How can I live in the now of each moment, without worrying about the past or future?

REVERSED

This can be an indication that you are putting too much pressure on yourself, striving to reach a state of perfection. Perhaps an idealized sense of reality is preventing you from experiencing the blessings in the now, as you strive for the future without pausing to relax. This can also indicate a sense of dissatisfaction or disruption in your life due to past experiences. Perhaps there is a lack of harmony or connection with others. How are your thoughts supporting you at this time? Take some time to reconnect with the people in your life or the activities or experiences you may be putting off. It may be an opportune time to ground yourself and prioritize what you really want.

PAGE OF CUPS

Keys: imaginative • youthful • free • emotional • sentimental
• sensitivity • romance • inspiration • intuition

PAGE OF CUPS

Crouched at the edge of a great ocean, a young woman offers a reflective, intuitive message. She is very much aware of our feelings, how we are doing in this moment, and whether we are harboring some kind of emotional blockage. This power of awareness comes to her naturally, and she gives it away freely without expectation. There is a universal, cosmic force that runs through her, driving her creativity and deliverance of wisdom.

THE MESSAGE

A time to check in with your spiritual voice and nature. Trust your intuition and feelings—you are on the right path. This is the beginning phase of a new adventure, project, or idea. Take this time to work through your creative processes; they will guide you more than you know.

PEOPLE

The Page of Cups is a kind, romantic individual who is highly intuitive and sensitive to others. When they show up in your life, expect to see the world through an entirely new lens. They tend to have a strong inner wisdom that baffles most people. This can also be reflected in the lifestyles they choose to align with. To some, these individuals can seem a bit aloof or disconnected from reality; perhaps they choose not to conform to society or have strange occupations or habits. This type might also have trouble finding their tribe. When they do make connections, however, they bond for life and never look back. The Page of Cups embodies a sort of ethereal magic that comes from celebrating their Inner Child and wants you to feel and explore this quality in yourself.

QUESTIONS TO ASK

⚠ How am I connecting with my creativity and spiritual nature?

⚠ Is it time for me to take a break from the stress of my daily life?

REVERSED

A lack of maturity or direction. Someone who might be emotionally on edge. As a result, they may choose various outlets for escapism or self-indulgence. A creative outlet could be needed in order to release any shadowed energies. A time for healing.

KNIGHT OF CUPS

Keys: feminine • artistic • romantic • bearer of good news
• youth • enthusiasm • adventure • impulsiveness

Standing at the edge of an ancient doorway, a woman mentally prepares for a journey into the great unknown. She has set her mind in motion, imagining her days ahead without any worry for what might await her on the other side. Once she steps through, there is no turning back. The water behind her embodies the dreamy, impulsive nature of her quest—a call for action beyond her current understanding. Drawn forward, she relies purely on her intuition and psychic abilities.

THE MESSAGE

The arrival of great news, an invitation, or an adventure. New experiences are on the horizon: ones that will emotionally nourish your soul and heart. The pursuit and manifestation of creative ventures or projects. Being able to identify the necessary steps to reach your goals.

PEOPLE

The Knight of Cups is one of the dreamiest cards of the Tarot. This person embodies an aptitude for adventure that defies all reason and logic. In love with the concept of love, the Knight of Cups will also go above and beyond when it comes to fulfilling their partner's needs. They can, however, become obsessive and overly sensitive, placing too much thought or worry onto words or emotions. Due to their passionate personalities, they tend to draw others to them easily. The Knight of Cups will always make decisions based on what their heart is telling them, whether their choices seem logical or not. Expect lots of passion, play, and adventure with this type.

QUESTIONS TO ASK

⚠ Am I harboring feelings toward someone in my life?

⚠ Am I ready to make a concrete plan with my new venture or project?

REVERSED

Erratic emotions, sometimes stemming from jealousy or resentment. A sense of suspicion caused by a loss of inner power or self-love. Emotional neediness or a tendency to react emotionally rather than logically. Initial hopes or aspirations may end in disappointment.

QUEEN OF CUPS

Keys: introspective • psychic • loving • compassionate
• honest • healing • empathetic

QUEEN OF CUPS

The Queen of Cups looks directly into the deepest corners of our hearts. She is dreamy and intuitive and aligns with the divine principle of love, being a channel of light in all that she does. In her realm, we see the stars of the cosmos above her, a sacred mirror of her connection to Source energy. From a deep place of knowing, she lives her life with a sense of care for all who cross her path, always putting others before herself.

THE MESSAGE

This card comes as an opportunity to nurture your relationships with others and to make time for celebratory gatherings. Listen to your inner voice and psychic abilities. The manifestation of loving energy and soulful experiences with the people in your life. Creativity and expression in all of its glory.

PEOPLE

The Queen of Cups is a nurturing individual who is deeply attuned to the needs of others. Her warm and tender personality will make you feel at home from the moment you meet her, and she gives advice freely and unconditionally, with love. This woman is real and won't bother with small talk or formalities, so expect to connect with her on the deepest of levels. It's not uncommon for the Queen of Cups to be a natural healer, working her magic subconsciously through her creations or in actual mystical or spiritual practices. The Queen of Cups expresses a deep wisdom from the unseen realms of spiritual insight (and may even have the ability to see into the spirit world). She might appear quiet and shy but is highly intelligent and strong in her convictions. Remember to be gentle with her heart, for she hurts easily.

QUESTIONS TO ASK

⚠ How can I put aside some time that is just for me?
⚠ Am I ready to explore my own interests, passions, and creative outlets?

REVERSED

There may be some kind of difficulty in expressing feelings or emotions. A tendency toward escapism or detachment from others. An involuntary need to take on other people's energies, whether positive or negative. An emotional empath who may pick up attachments from negative situations.

KING OF CUPS

Keys: nurturing • emotional • psychic • wise • strong
• sensitive • diplomatic • generous • stable

KING OF CUPS

Standing in a great ocean, the King of Cups finds his energy to be both grounded and connected in this space. In each hand he holds a cup, the perfect balance of the unconscious and conscious realms, which are fully at his disposal. The water beneath him supplies him with an endless force of creative and intuitive potential, as he is at one with this element and works with it freely with the confidence of self-mastery.

THE MESSAGE

This card points to emotions and intuitive strengths and how they have the power to change or influence our lives. It denotes an ability to balance creativity and artistic expression with knowledge and wisdom and speaks of the connection between your inner voice and Higher Self.

PEOPLE

The most sensitive and psychic of all the Kings, this individual is ruled by both head and heart. A natural leader, he exudes a sense of diplomacy and awareness that seems to illustrate his control over his emotions, but, underneath the surface, he is highly sensitive. The King of Cups also knows how to celebrate life and enjoys making time for fun and creativity, letting loose when he needs to. When it comes to the sad side of the King of Cups, there may be an indication of lost opportunities, heartache, or flaky behavior. This type can become lost in a world of self-made fantasies, either wanting to escape through self-indulgence or in pretending that everything is A-OK when it's clearly not. This King needs extra support and can hurt those around him if he is not able to balance all of his responsibilities and creative outlets properly.

QUESTIONS TO ASK

⚠ How can I find balance at this time?

⚠ How can I reach out and make time with the people I love?

REVERSED

A suspicion of others, letting the imagination take over. Someone who may be deceptive, manipulative, or lost in fantasy. An irrational state of thinking caused by past attachments. A need to release negative associations and heal within. A need for more self-love and positive self-expression.

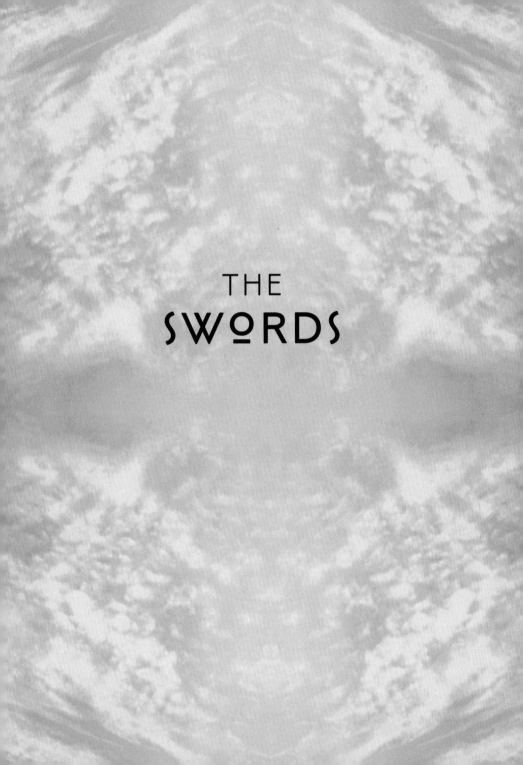

THE
SWORDS

ACE OF SWORDS

Keys: beginning • clarity • joy • victory • determination
• power • justice • honesty

ACE OF SWORDS

On the first card of this strong suit, we see the shape of a sword, ready to be wielded to its full potential. How will you use this newfound power? The Ace of Swords cuts through all illusion, seeking out truth, reason, and objectivity. The appearance of this card prompts you to explore the expression of some kind of hidden message or inspiration that needs to be brought to light.

THE MESSAGE

The Ace of Swords indicates a heightened state of spiritual and mental clarity. It marks the emergence of great determination and power in order to reach your goals successfully. It signifies a new beginning, project, plan, or vision. Very often, this also connects with an accelerated shift in consciousness, as you are able to move ahead with wisdom and truth. It may feel as though nothing can stop this progress, regardless of what the future may hold. Now is the time to seize opportunities in order to create positive new changes in your life. A time to stand out on your own, against all odds.

QUESTIONS TO ASK

⚠ Am I ready to move through this new phase of life with a clear direction?

⚠ Do I need to face some hidden truth or facts at this time?

REVERSED

You may be disconnected from reaching your highest potential if you are not aware of where your gifts truly lie. Low-vibrational thoughts may be manifesting into your reality, or there may be obstacles in the way. A need to face a truth or confront inner desires. An ideal time for deep meditation and introspection with regard to life passions, goals, and priorities.

TWO OF SWORDS

Keys: equilibrium • peace and justice • truth • self-doubt
• strength • illumination • denial

TWO OF SWORDS

Standing here before a mountainous landscape, a woman looks out into the world ahead. At her sides are two swords placed in the sand, representing a division between her direction and mindset. As she considers the options, her avoidance of making a decision prevents her from moving forward.

THE MESSAGE

If you find yourself at a crossroads, there may be a need to find a sense of balance between two or more opposing factors in your life. Generally when this card shows up, we are experiencing some sort of difficulty in making a concrete plan or decision about something. Perhaps we feel numb or are ignorant of the entirety of the situation and cannot see what is unraveling around us. It is time to acknowledge the situation head-on in order to process what you have been avoiding. Do not fear the potential outcomes, as fear will only hold you back from finding a positive solution. Have the courage to trust in yourself, and your path will become clear. Once you are able to make a choice, your confidence and strength will soar to new heights.

QUESTIONS TO ASK

⚠ Am I ready to focus my intent and energy into one direction at this time?

⚠ What am I holding on to that is preventing me from moving forward?

REVERSED

When reversed, the Two of Swords can be an indication of some kind of self-delusion or illusory mindset that prevents you from connecting with the intentions of your heart, as if you were blind to the truth. (In traditional decks, the figure on this card is often blindfolded.) If there is someone in your life whom you need to reconnect with, now might be an opportune moment to reach out. This card can also express feelings of being overwhelmed by options, views, opinions, or ideas. A fear of potential consequences or outcomes. If you find yourself stuck in the middle of a quarrel or argument, it might be a good idea to remove yourself quietly in order to find a way to release the negative energies or attachments. It is time to do what is solely right for you.

THREE OF SWORDS

Keys: heartbreak • obstacles • redirection of negative forces
• sacrifice • loss • learning • healing

THREE OF SWORDS

Standing in quiet contemplation, a woman thinks about her present situation. There is a sense of sadness, loneliness, and possible heartbreak. She wonders how she will be able to move forward and heal the hurt she is experiencing. Around her are three swords driven into the ground, holding her captive within her anguish. Between her hands floats the shape of a full moon, representing the push and pull of her emotions.

THE MESSAGE

A more ominous card than most, the Three of Swords often reflects moments of loss, pain, betrayal, or heartache—either within your own experience or because you are causing pain to someone else. Although the presence of such obstacles may feel overwhelming, very often a greater lesson will emerge out of the darkness. From these fragments of shadow come the clarity and potential to create new opportunities. How we face adversity can have a lifelong effect on our happiness and consciousness if we habitually choose to focus on the negative. Your innate strength and wisdom will emerge as you realize your full potential to learn and grow from past mistakes or challenges. You alone have the power to rise above the obscurity to reach a higher state of awareness.

QUESTIONS TO ASK

⚠ Am I ready to move forward and work through the shadows that have been inflicted in my life?

⚠ Are there any painful memories or experiences from my past that I am still holding on to?

REVERSED

You are emerging out of a negative phase of your life. There is light at the end of the tunnel, and now you must continue to move forward. You have acknowledged your pain and have been able to process it into a positive learning experience. From this new stage, you are ready to see the world through a new lens. If there are, conversely, dark or negative influences in your life that have been present for too long, it may be a good time to face these and prepare yourself for some kind of acknowledgment and release. Know that love is not only still present in your life, it will begin to reveal itself increasingly as you heal within.

FOUR OF SWORDS

Keys: rest • relaxation • entertainment • hobbies • solitude
• reevaluation • meditation • recovery

Standing here at the edge of another world, a woman glances back in quiet reflection, thinking about how far she has come. After one last moment of contemplation, she feels it is time to pause and rest. Knowing that she may still have a long journey ahead of her, she takes this temporary interlude as an opportunity to recalibrate her energies before preparing for her next move.

THE MESSAGE

The Four of Swords often highlights a time to retreat from the stress and chaos of the world. If you have been experiencing any setbacks or difficulties, take a moment to reflect and meditate on the issues at hand. You will need this time to recuperate and revitalize yourself in order to face or resolve any potential challenges that may return. This pause could offer you a fresh perspective and allow you to process the experience without feeling too pressured or rushed. Give yourself this time to recover and prepare yourself mentally for the journey ahead. After this, you may feel clearer about how things will ultimately unfold once you have a better sense of how to use your energies. A wonderful time for introspection and self-exploration.

QUESTIONS TO ASK

⚠ How can I make time for relaxation?

⚠ What potential challenges can I mentally prepare myself for at this time?

REVERSED

A sense of nervousness or loss of stability as you are overburdened by responsibilities or choices. Feeling stagnant and frustrated with the lack of direction or progress at this time. Perhaps you have not been making enough time for healthy choices. How can you be more active in making positive changes in your life? Have your dreams been hypothetical, or have you taken the necessary steps to manifest them fully? You may need to acknowledge certain negative energies in order to move forward with relief or closure.

FIVE OF SWORDS

Keys: defeat • loss • disillusionment • gossip • mistrust
• selfishness • ego • disagreements

Standing in a shadowy landscape, a woman ponders the complexity of her situation. Surrounding her are five swords, each a representation of her own disarming powers. Despite her victory, she is not feeling triumphant or positive in her situation. There is a sense of restlessness and emptiness in her heart.

THE MESSAGE

The Five of Swords indicates a state of entrapment or negativity that has been self-inflicted. Through conflict, disagreements, or impulsive behavior, there has been an involuntary burdening of yourself or others. This card highlights pointless winning and needing to be right regardless of the outcome. This comes at a high cost and can alienate you from the people around you. It is important to step back and take a look at the bigger picture. Put everything into perspective and realize where your true priorities and truths lie. Are your opinions and views more important than your relationships? How are you affecting other people? Is your ambition coming from a place of love or fear? How can your words and actions transform this difficult situation?

QUESTIONS TO ASK

⚠ Am I ready to connect with my heart's true intentions?

⚠ Am I being forced onto an uncomfortable path?

REVERSED

A shift in negative energy to one of positive change. A need for closure before being able to move forward. Fears associated with past traumas or memories. Unresolved issues. It could be that others do not agree with the direction you are heading in. Stand strong and listen to your inner voice. Do not let the negative thoughts or opinions of others affect you.

SIX OF SWORDS

Keys: new adventures • travel • recovery • success after turmoil
• sacrifice • change

Poised before a great mountain, a woman looks ahead, mentally preparing herself for what is to come. Although she is slightly uncertain about how things will unfold, she is confident that whatever awaits her beyond this final ascent will be better than what she is leaving behind.

THE MESSAGE

The Six of Swords often shows up during times of transition and change; these might involve a move, travel, or upcoming events that mark new opportunities. This card may also highlight the need to let go of something, or some kind of sacrifice that must take place in order to move forward. This could be a difficult choice to make, but know that it is merely a transitory phase and you will benefit in the long run. With time, you may come to understand the advantage of letting things go as part of an evolutionary process. It is the acceptance of change and release in order to grow from experience. After moving on, you will be able to reflect on your path and the choices you have made. The Six of Swords is a card of progress, evolution, and new developments.

QUESTIONS TO ASK

⚠ Am I ready to take this next leap forward?

⚠ Have I come to terms with my past?

REVERSED

Although you know that change is inevitable and will likely lead to a more positive route, you may still be experiencing attachments that you are not ready to let go of. It may feel as though a force is preventing you from reaching your Higher Self. Know that you alone have the power to shift your energy onto a new course. You are strong enough to navigate and face life's challenges at every turn.

SEVEN OF SWORDS

Keys: over-confidence • deception • selfishness
• secrecy • betrayal • subterfuge

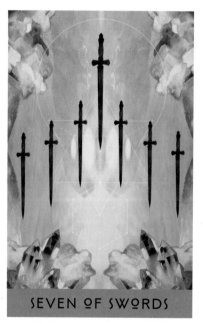

SEVEN OF SWORDS

As one of the sneakiest cards in the Tarot, the Seven of Swords speaks of duplicitous behavior, dishonesty, and secrets that are self-serving. This comes at a high cost and speaks of actions that must be faced. When this card appears in a reading, it may also indicate a hidden message that must be exposed and revealed.

THE MESSAGE

The Seven of Swords often illustrates a challenge that may be associated with some kind of dishonesty, deceit, or illusion, whether on the part of yourself or someone else. It can indicate an avoidance of truth, with consequences that become apparent when least expected. If there is some kind of secrecy taking place, a new approach or solution is highly encouraged. Omitting the truth is never a good idea, especially if a positive outcome is desired. It is also advised that you remain cautious with others who may not have your best interests at heart. Perhaps now is the time to lay out everything on the table and communicate from a place of frank honesty. A time for clarity and truth.

QUESTIONS TO ASK

⚠ Am I hiding something that may potentially hurt someone I know?

⚠ Is there some energy or force that is currently exerting pressure on me at this time?

REVERSED

A need to acknowledge the challenges in order to move forward. A time for letting go of self-doubt or any attachments that are preventing opportunities in your life. Know that you are capable of anything you wish to achieve, so it is important not to limit yourself with worry or insecurity. This is a time to look at the situation head-on in order to see where you stand. Light glimmers on the far horizon.

EIGHT OF SWORDS

Keys: helplessness • disempowerment • choice
• perspective • isolation • restriction

EIGHT OF SWORDS

Slumped in defeat, a young woman finds herself encircled with swords and believes herself to be enclosed and bound to where she rests. Unable to get up, she is feeling overburdened and helpless. Here, she cannot see the light of the world around her and does not know that she has the power and freedom to escape her situation.

THE MESSAGE

The Eight of Swords suggests an inability to move forward due to a clouded perception. This may be a strong indication that despite your fear or sense of helplessness, there is a positive solution available to you. You may need to step out of this negative space in order to see the light that surrounds you. How are you processing your energy and thoughts? Fear-based thinking may limit your view of the world and keep you in a state of entrapment. If you feel affected by external circumstances (or other people), know that you alone have the power to make a change. It is important to remember that you cannot control the thoughts or views of others, but you can control how you think and react. You can choose whether to be disempowered or to be strong and limitless in your potential.

QUESTIONS TO ASK

⚠ How can I see through the obscurity around me?

⚠ Is there some way I can shift my perspective of this challenging situation?

REVERSED

A state of acceptance and responsibility for yourself. Learning from past mistakes, traumas, and circumstances. The need to process emotional blockages in order to make positive changes. You understand the benefit of loving intentions in all areas of your life and how negative attachments to issues or others only exacerbates the challenges along the way.

NINE OF SWORDS

Keys: fear • illusion • despair • isolation • anxiety • depression • worry • guilt

Finding herself in a dark landscape, a woman dwells amid the shadows of her thoughts. She is burdened with worry, unable to come to terms with her anguish. As a last resort, she holds on to one of her swords for strength, hoping that tomorrow will bring new light and opportunities.

THE MESSAGE

The Nine of Swords indicates a state of inner disharmony and habitual worrying that may manifest as anxiety, insomnia, or psychological fear. It can point to deceits of the imagination that are hindering your overall health and perspective. Things might not necessarily be as bad as you think, or perhaps you are being too hard on yourself. It may be time to seek counsel or connect with the people who love and support you. If there is an issue that is bothering you, address it head-on in order to hold space for greater healing. This card may also indicate that it is important for you to stop worrying about the views or opinions of others. Know that you deserve to be happy and that a positive outcome is closer than you think.

QUESTIONS TO ASK

⚠ How can I look to the root of my worries in order to bring light and illumination to my situation?

⚠ Are there burdens or memories from my past that are still causing pain or hurt in my life?

REVERSED

Things may be blown out of proportion, limiting your perspective on life. It could be that the negative forces in your life have reached an apex and that you are now causing yet more harm to yourself and your overall health. How can you rise above the stress you are experiencing? Your state of despair is not healthy and can only cause more pain in the long run. Take a deep breath and broaden your approach to this situation. It may be that, very soon, all of this will be behind you. It is time to make a positive change. Do not be afraid to ask for help.

TEN OF SWORDS

Keys: recovery • enlightenment • release • transformation
• tipping point • hurt

TEN OF SWORDS

The Ten of Swords indicates the end of a cycle and a new beginning. To continue along a path toward a newfound enlightenment, some kind of sacrifice or internal release may be necessary. This could mean having to take the hit of a final challenge before progressing to the next stage, or coming to terms with an inevitable loss or hardship.

THE MESSAGE

The Ten of Swords may appear during difficult life challenges that are traumatic, disastrous, or unexpected. It can also be an indication of lying or deceit on the part of someone else, with the hurtful outcome of feeling betrayed. Know that despite the hardships, a new phase or beginning will transpire. By processing and releasing this phase of your life, you will learn to move forward with illumination and strength. It marks the transformation of negative experiences that puts everything else into perspective, in seeing past the shadows to the light that shines through.

QUESTIONS TO ASK

⚠ How can I seek out support at this time?

⚠ Is there something that I need to process that I have been holding on to?

REVERSED

It is important to acknowledge all of the fears and the pain that have been affecting your life. Are you still holding on to grief or hurtful memories from your past? It could be that you will need to face things from many years ago that are still unresolved that act as roots to the many layers of your anguish. After you have done this, give yourself permission to acknowledge and heal the emotional wounds in order to make room for new opportunities and perspectives. This practice of self-love may also stem from a need to forgive yourself or others.

PAGE OF SWORDS

Keys: enthusiastic • knowledgeable • logical • passionate

PAGE OF SWORDS

Standing beneath the phases of the moon, the Page of Swords presents you with an honest truth; her hands are outstretched, proffering that which you might not yet be able to see or comprehend. At her sides rest a number of swords—representations of her acute ability to pierce through all illusion.

THE MESSAGE

A renewed sense of vitality and energy is on the horizon. Now is the time to move forward with your plans, regardless of the thoughts or views of those around you. The Page of Swords represents the beginning phase or initial steps of a venture or project. Do not be afraid to take a leap into the unknown—there is magic ahead!

PEOPLE

A perceptive and discerning individual who is highly ambitious. This person absorbs information like a sponge and is capable of understanding highly complex ideas. The Page of Swords lives by a code of truth and frank honesty, which makes them excellent speakers, writers, and teachers. Their sharp minds are fantastic mechanisms for objective communication and planning when it comes to their life choices, but they tend to be a bit reserved in their personalities, generally siding with logic and reason over spontaneous thinking. Despite their intellectualism, they may need more life experience in order to discern between their logical mind and spiritual self, and they may find it challenging to be faced with free souls who are emotionally expressive. When surrounded by other elements (such as watery Cups or fiery Wands), they are more likely to come out of their shells.

QUESTIONS TO ASK

⚠ Am I ready and open to receive any new invitations and opportunities that come my way?

⚠ Am I ready to speak my own truth and express myself more?

REVERSED

Someone who is full of great ideas and plans but has difficulty manifesting them into reality. A need to review any necessary steps concerning whatever has been expressed and discussed, or else disappointment may occur.

KNIGHT OF SWORDS

Keys: ambitious • capable • energetic • self-determined
• abrasive • honest • critical • impetuous

KNIGHT OF SWORDS

Crouched at the edge of a rocky ledge, the Knight of Swords prepares herself for the ultimate leap. She is mentally unaffected by her environment, completely driven and motivated to forge her own path into the portal below her. At her side rests her sword, a symbol for the sharp awareness and self-assurance that she carries within her wherever she goes.

THE MESSAGE

You have clear intentions, and your eye is on the prize. It is, however, important that you make a clear plan for those necessary steps in order to reach your goals. Do not move too hastily or rush ahead, or else you may find that you will be regretful.

PEOPLE

An enthusiastic, assertive individual who is both intelligent and energetic. The Knight of Swords views the world around them as a playground of opportunities, possibly seeing themselves as superior to others or to systems of authority. This type sets high standards for their own goals, working to the brink of their potential and endurance. This can appear intimidating to others, as not many people can live up to this high level of intensity or demand. They may appear antisocial, curt, or abrasive, alienating themselves without care. They are ready to take any necessary steps to manifest their desires, which can sometimes make them seem hasty or impulsive. Often demonstrating a minor lack of foresight but great determination in achieving what they want.

QUESTIONS TO ASK

⚠ How am I balancing my life at this time?

⚠ What is the ultimate end goal that I am working toward?

REVERSED

A sense of impatience or impulsivity. The Knight of Swords reversed is indicative of a mind that races a hundred miles a minute with an endless flow of energy. Even though there may be great ideas, hopes, and aspirations, there is a need for organization and planning. This card can also indicate a state of rebelliousness and naive risk taking. Gaining life experience through making mistakes may be a necessary evil.

QUEEN OF SWORDS

Keys: independent • perfectionist • intellectual • articulate
• impartial • honest

QUEEN OF SWORDS

The Queen of Swords sits here at the border of a great expanse. She is very wise, having built the life she's envisioned through her own cunning and perceptive strength. In her hand she holds her sword, a tribute to and symbol of her high intellect. At her side lies a large feline, the representation of her authoritative will and mental prowess.

THE MESSAGE

Your strength and powers of discernment are needed at this time. You may want to detach your inner emotions or fears from your given situation in order to make an objective decision. Look to all the facts before making any judgments.

PEOPLE

An incredibly insightful, quick-witted person, the Queen of Swords is able to see through illusion and deception, speaking her truth at any given time. Highly perceptive, analytical, and straightforward, she embodies a deep maturity that only comes through life experience. She has been through a lot, knows how to use her time wisely, and has refined her to-do list and schedule with mastery. This also points to how she has taken control over her mind and thoughts: There is no point in wobbling over spilled milk; better just to clean it up and move on. Not an especially emotional type, the Queen of Swords connects with others through her sharp intellectualism, bonding for life with the people who "get" her. When she is on your side, she is extremely loyal and supportive, despite her apparent coldness, and is aware of the importance of your connection.

QUESTIONS TO ASK

⚠ How can I connect with my strength of discernment?

⚠ How can I look at things objectively, with compassion?

REVERSED

When reversed, this card highlights the importance of your intuitive and emotional strengths rather than relying solely on logic, or, conversely, using the intellect over emotion. The Queen of Swords reversed may also indicate impassivity and indifference when it comes to dealing with other people, or an overall lack of communication.

KING OF SWORDS

Keys: authority • logic • reason • ambition • honor
• confidence • strength • analysis

KING OF SWORDS

The King of Swords stands at the base of a great mountain, acutely aware of his surroundings. Reflected by his face are two mirrored images of his persona, a representation of his worldly knowledge and discernment of thought, intellect, and communication. He knows exactly what to do and say in any given situation, sourcing his wisdom from personal experience and pure logic.

THE MESSAGE

It is time to speak your truth with confidence and strength. The need to look objectively with no limiting emotions. You are quick witted and sharp in your convictions, standing up against all odds. Do not concern yourself with the opinions of others. You already know you have what it takes.

PEOPLE

The King of Swords is an intelligent, decisive individual who handles his life logically at all times. Often seen as a person of authority, he knows exactly how to get things done and excludes emotional expression and spontaneity from his lifestyle. Since he tends to be less sensitive, his way of connecting with the people he loves may come from a place of rational thinking rather than sweet sentimentality. He may also appear harsh or insensitive, unaware of how his curt communication or tone of voice affects those around him, even though he isn't necessarily coming from a place of negativity. Despite his flaws, he is firm and fair and is able to express good judgment at all times. The King of Swords is also very inventive and may be responsible for many of the scientific breakthroughs and engineering developments of our time.

QUESTIONS TO ASK

⚠ How can I approach my given situation from a place of clear objectivity?
⚠ How are my actions, thoughts, or words affecting those around me?

REVERSED

The manipulation of authority, intelligence, or power. It could reflect someone who is egotistical, cruel, and selfish, who takes things personally and expects the worst from others. In another light, this card can indicate the need to be more firm, direct, and decisive in personal convictions. A need for organization, clarity, and direction.

THE
CRYSTALS
(PENTACLES)

ACE OF CRYSTALS

Keys: prosperity • stability • possessions • opportunities
• new ventures • fertility • rewards

ACE OF CRYSTALS

As the first card of this transformational suit, the Ace of Crystals stands strong amid a colorful, sparkling backdrop. A great omen to receive! This abundant energy speaks of new beginnings that are filled with tangible results and positive investments. Whether it be a new project or idea, now is the time to take action!

THE MESSAGE

The Ace of Crystals signifies a new and prosperous beginning that has the potential to grow into long-term success. If you are contemplating some kind of business venture or investment, now may be a good time to set things in motion. The energy of this card speaks of planning and strategizing—laying out the blueprint for the foreseeable future, knowing that the outcome will be fruitful and positive. From this state of understanding comes the ability to identify opportunities as they arise and those routes that align best with your heart. This card speaks of the innate trust, intuition, and choices that support spiritual growth. You understand and prioritize what is truly important and are able to rally all of the resources you need along the way. If this card points to areas in your life other than finances, use it as an indication of sparks of inspiration and action there too. Remember, the power of positive visualization combined with a sense of gratitude will only attract more abundance into your life.

QUESTIONS TO ASK

⚠ Am I considering an important step for my future?

⚠ How can I use my own creativity to build something new?

REVERSED

When reversed, the Ace of Crystals can point to some kind of loss or financial risk. Be careful with your money and how you choose to spend it. The appearance of this card can indicate exploitation or greed on the part of yourself or someone else and advises caution. It signifies the burden of excessive materialism or a lack of deep spiritual insight. There may be a need to rethink your priorities and to reevaluate a certain approach.

TWO OF CRYSTALS

Keys: progress • balance • transition • priorities
• goals • flexibility • adaptability

As an energetic portal of insight, the Two of Crystals represents a foreseeable light ahead. There is a balanced structure in this card: The options are visible, the developments are clear, and the possibilities endless. As you look at this image, think about how you can harness your power and sheer will in order to balance your goals and dreams. There is much to look forward to!

THE MESSAGE

The Two of Crystals often highlights those moments in life that require a bit of juggling and adaptability. When tasks, responsibilities, obligations, scheduling, and everything in between tend to pull us in a million different directions, the Two of Crystals asks how we can find a happy balance amid these active forces. It's not impossible; it may just require a little bit of planning and inner self-confidence. Sometimes this card also points to future goals that will need to be taken into consideration as you transition from one stage of your life into the next. For all that you have accomplished, you should continue to move forward and be proud of your success but not forget to acknowledge the other important, meaningful aspects of your life. This could mean connections with friends and family members or the activities you love and enjoy.

QUESTIONS TO ASK

⚠ How can I find a sense of balance at this time?

⚠ How can I continue to devote time to my passions and interests?

REVERSED

When reversed, the Two of Crystals can speak of feeling overwhelmed by too many responsibilities or choices. In order to find some semblance of balance, it may be necessary to cut out some of the pressures in your life or to find some kind of support system. Perhaps you will need to step back and take a quiet interlude in which to recalibrate your thoughts and energies. It could be that your health and mental state are being affected. A need to balance work, love, play, health, and spirituality.

THREE OF CRYSTALS

Keys: skill • originality • determination • career
• artistry • collaboration • cooperation

A young woman stands next to the powerful form of a cheetah; between them, there is a shared synergy of magic and respect. Here, their combined energies create a strength and spiritual fortitude that connect them throughout lifetimes. Framing the head of the young woman, three crystals circulate, a representation of completion and the cycles of change.

THE MESSAGE

The Three of Crystals highlights the sacred magic and union that come with collaboration, teamwork, and the ability to support and identify individual strengths. The arrival of this card may also be an indication that you have reached a state of accomplishment after all of your hard work and, with your newfound insight, you understand the steps you need to take in order to maintain the momentum of your success. This card also signifies great skill, passion, and the manifestation of creative projects, either through your own efforts or with the help of another person or group of individuals. After what you have learned, you are not someone who comes off as superior to others; rather, you appreciate the qualities and strengths that each person has to offer: a great sense of wisdom, spiritual enlightenment, and modesty, which comes through the embodiment of unconditional love.

QUESTIONS TO ASK

⚠ How can I combine my energies and creativity with those around me who also support my visions or dreams?

⚠ Are there any projects I am working on that may require a bit of help?

REVERSED

When reversed, the Three of Crystals may signify an obsessive or controlling mindset that prevents the proper execution or manifestation of a particular goal or plan. Perhaps there is also an element of insecurity, due to a fear of what others think. A need to look outside the box to gain a broader perspective. Now may be a good time to make some concrete plans. Take a moment to meditate on your priorities and make a list of what you can do to help your situation. A time for change and new beginnings.

FOUR OF CRYSTALS

Keys: possessiveness • obstacles • greed • resistance to change • control • materialism

In the shadowy confinement of a cave, a young man sits in possession of his earthly treasures: four crystals of materialistic value and power. Here, he basks in the shining light from above, focusing all of his energy on what he retains in this narrow space.

THE MESSAGE

Although you have reached a wonderful state of success, it may be a good time to take a closer look at your priorities. Are you spending too much time focusing on personal affluence or materialistic things, such as possessions, the accumulation of wealth, or social status? You should continue to take pride in all that you have achieved but not let the illusion of physical wealth get in the way of who you really are. This card can also point to a desire for stability, settling down, or a conservative lifestyle that prevents any risk-taking behavior. It can also reflect hoarding or negative attachments that stunt personal growth or change. Is there an emotional void you are trying to fill by holding on to things that mask a lack of security in your life?

QUESTIONS TO ASK

⚠ Am I ready to look beyond the materialistic values of my life?

⚠ If I lost all of my assets and physical possessions, what would I consider to be important thereafter?

REVERSED

When reversed, the Four of Crystals may be an indication of excessive materialism or a fear of poverty. It could also mean you are spending too much time focusing on work and not prioritizing your energy in a healthy way. Try spending some time either by yourself or with the people you love. An opportune time to maintain balance—or else important opportunities or experiences may go unnoticed.

FIVE OF CRYSTALS

Keys: worry • over-speculation • loss • manifestation
• lack • hardship

As one of the more sorrowful cards of the Tarot, the Five of Crystals speaks of loss, worry, or hardship that may show up in various manifestations in your life. Here we see the forms of five crystals floating in front of a cosmic doorway—indicating heavy burdens of the mind that block and impede our advancement and well-being.

THE MESSAGE

The Five of Crystals tends to show up when we are experiencing some kind of worry or loss. It could indicate an actual state of illness, a lack of finances, or a feeling of rejection. Very often, this leaves us with a sense of nonfulfillment, as if something very important is missing. Perhaps we have lost a friend, a loved one, a pet, a job, or a sense of security that once made us feel whole and capable. Over time, if we continue to dwell in this stressful mindset, we can accumulate feelings of helplessness and victimhood and may become codependent on others. Know that, despite the hardships you may be experiencing, there is still hope and support available. You have the power to come out of this situation in a new and positive light. Help might be closer than you think—is there a friend, loved one, counselor, or person you trust whom you can reach out to at this time? It might also be a good time to check your emotions: How are you manifesting your energy? Are you projecting your fears into your reality?

QUESTIONS TO ASK

⚠ How can I rise above the stress of this situation?

⚠ Is there a way I can reach out for help?

REVERSED

There is light at the end of the tunnel! Look ahead with a renewed sense of optimism, as you are now able to proceed with confidence and strength. An understanding of the cycles of your life; much like the Wheel of Fortune, this card indicates the passing or transition of one phase into the next.

SIX OF CRYSTALS

Keys: new opportunities • career • philanthropy • generosity
• prosperity • advancements • growth • abundance

Standing on a desert mountain, a woman is depicted here at two different levels. Above, she is seen basking in a celestial light with six encircling crystals, a positive portrayal of a stage in her life when things are going well and she is able to see above the stress of her previous hardship. Below, we see her crouched in a moment of shock, a contrast to her paralleled energy from above.

THE MESSAGE

The Six of Crystals indicates a state of balance and abundance in your life and comes as a very harmonious blessing. Whether you are in a position to be of service somehow and help someone in need or you are in a state of lack and need some kind of support, this card highlights the appearance of compassion and generosity. You recognize the value of your relationships, spirituality, and the mutual benefit of care and kindness with others. This is also a time for inner growth and prosperity. You have risen to the occasion and can now look back on the choices you made that have led to your higher state of awareness: How will you move up from here? Opportunities, gifts, or rewards may be closer than you think.

QUESTIONS TO ASK

⚠ How can I help those around me who may need additional support?

⚠ How can I open my heart and show gratitude in my life?

REVERSED

An imbalance of energies. If you are being generous with others in some way, be careful that you are not being taken advantage of. The Six of Crystals reversed may also indicate a need to maintain a sense of selflessness in your generosity. Are there hidden motives behind your actions, or are you working from a place of love? If this card pertains to relationships, it could be that there is an imbalance of energy between two people: Is someone giving more than the other?

SEVEN OF CRYSTALS

Keys: anticipation • contemplation • visions • intuition
• meditation • spiritual truth

Shown here in a desert landscape, a young woman meditates on what she has built and developed in her life. Above her hands float seven crystals, the energetic manifestations of her blessings and refined skills. As she ponders over her creations, she thinks about what she would like to achieve next, setting her mind to the task ahead.

THE MESSAGE

The Seven of Crystals indicates a new perspective relating to your life goals. It could be that you feel as though you have worked very hard but have yet to reap the rewards. Now is not the time to give up! If you are feeling stuck at the moment, take some time to rest and review your next steps. Perhaps you have learned more than you thought possible along the way and have shifted your priorities unexpectedly. It could simply be a matter of gaining a new perspective and trusting your instincts—mind, body, and spirit. Look at your life and think of everything you have accomplished and all that you are grateful for. This phase is simply a pause along your journey.

QUESTIONS TO ASK

△ Is there a greater lesson or goal that I wish to experience at this time?
△ How have I changed and grown?
△ What can I celebrate and be grateful for?

REVERSED

How are you using your energy at this time? Is it paying off, or are you becoming frustrated with the lack of output? This could be an indication that you are putting in everything you have, emotionally and mentally, yet are still not manifesting your plans. If this relates to a relationship, there might be an imbalance of some sort, and one person may end up being disappointed in the end.

EIGHT OF CRYSTALS

Keys: perseverance · ingenuity · spiritual growth · education · proficiency · craftsmanship · industry

EIGHT OF CRYSTALS

Shown here at the edge of a lush rainforest, a woman stands beneath the light of the cosmos, reveling in the crystals that float above her hands. She has dedicated time and effort in her life in order to reap the positive results of her craft and knows that inspiration and patience will be needed to continue the momentum of her success.

THE MESSAGE

The Eight of Crystals highlights the well-earned rewards that you have worked for up until this point. Now, you can finally take a moment to reflect on these, knowing you well deserve this pat on the back. The appearance of this card also indicates that your strong will, hard work, perseverance, and diligent mindfulness have created the foundations of the success you are now enjoying—so bask in this light, baby, you deserve it! It may also indicate a new discovery, task, project, or creative venture that could end up having an enduring presence in your life, requiring energy and focus, so use this time to plan your next move. This doesn't need to be stressful; see it as a newfound adventure! This card can also relate to formal training or education, taking your talents to new heights, and marks the self-determination that comes from mental clarity and focus. It denotes the maturity that emerges from expanding your spiritual awareness through the act of growing and learning.

QUESTIONS TO ASK

⚠ Am I ready to take the next evolutionary step in my career?

⚠ Is there some kind of craft or hobby that I am ready to take seriously?

REVERSED

This might be an indication that you are expending all of your energy in your work and are neglecting your relationships with others. Because of this, you may also be failing to make time for your personal interests and mental well-being. A need to think outside the box in order to gain new perspectives and insights. If you have been putting all of your energy into a project or idea that is not working out, try reprioritizing your plans. What are you getting out of this in the end? Can you explore an alternative approach to a problem? A need to make long-term goals and to find a sense of balance.

NINE OF CRYSTALS

Keys: retreat • stability • sensuality • comfort • accomplishment
• spiritual growth • refinement

NINE OF CRYSTALS

Standing here on the slope of a great mountain, a woman looks out into the beautiful space of the world, connecting with the celestial light that exists within and around her. At one with the elements, she rejoices in their multidimensional power of transmutation and abundance.

THE MESSAGE

A wonderful card, the Nine of Crystals represents the culmination of all your efforts and hard work. You have gained a great deal of insight and knowledge along your journey, which has led to your current heightened state of awareness. There is a spiritual satisfaction in this card in that it speaks of those grand moments that stand out in life, which you will recall with total clarity and nostalgia when you are old and gray. Through the exploration and manifestation of your dreams, you have found your place in the universe and are radiating joy. Perhaps you will want to spend more time in nature or with the people you love. Perhaps you will take a more spiritual route in your learning. You are aware of the greater scope of your being and are ready to move on to the next phase of enlightenment. A time to enjoy life's simple pleasures.

QUESTIONS TO ASK

△   Am I ready to receive the rewards that I have worked for?

△   How can I now identify what my greatest skills and talents are?

REVERSED

An overindulgence in the physical or materialistic aspects of life. Working too hard toward goals without a proper payoff. The inability to reach a state of happiness or comfort if risks have been taken along the way. It may be necessary to take a step back and make a concrete plan. Again, this can come back to an imbalance in how your energies are being used. What can you shift or release? Are you ready to make a small sacrifice for growth?

TEN OF CRYSTALS

Keys: culmination • family • prosperity • security
• spiritual ascension • happiness

A beautiful card to receive, the Ten of Crystals is a tribute to all that we have worked toward. This card forms the dreamy backdrop of a place where you can go to bring offerings, light incense and candles, and express gratitude for this incredible chapter in your life. Here, we see how far we have come, while looking back on our journey with love and appreciation.

THE MESSAGE

The Ten of Crystals is a card of positive reflection and appreciation. It speaks of those times when the success of your journey becomes apparent with age, when you begin to experience the benefits of a life well lived. At this apex of light and stability, it is clear that you have built a strong foundation on which to rest and reap the benefits of everything you have worked toward. It is an indication of many blessings within your home, family, and future endeavors. Take this time to experience the freedom you have created for yourself. Enjoy life's simple pleasures, but don't forget to be generous with the knowledge or wealth you have gained.

QUESTIONS TO ASK

⚠ Am I ready to celebrate with my soul family and accept each moment as a gift?

⚠ As I look back on my life, can I take a moment to reflect on all of the incredible memories?

REVERSED

This card reversed can highlight those aspects of convention or security that keep us trapped in a rigid mindset. This could be due to the ingrained beliefs we have held for years, such as clinging to the idea that money equates with stability and protection. Very often, these attitudes mask a greater emotional void in our life. On another note, it may indicate an actual lack of security or stability unrelated to finances. It could be that you may need to start afresh and build up stronger foundations before reaching a sense of fulfillment or completion. Are you pursuing what truly makes you happy? How are your relationships with the people you love? What are your long-term goals?

PAGE OF CRYSTALS

Keys: entrepreneurial • dedicated • visionary • adept
• practical • positive omen

Standing at the edge of a dreamy landscape, the Page of Crystals is a messenger of great opportunity and blessings ahead. There is a dedication in her wisdom in that she knows how to manifest freely due to her ingenuity and spiritual foresight yet she is still in the early stages of who she will grow into as she learns and evolves over time.

THE MESSAGE

Your ideas and plans are headed in the right direction, so it is important to maintain a focus on your goals and aspirations. Now is the time to make concrete plans and to take action. The transition phase between dreams and reality. Expansion. Good news.

PEOPLE

The Page of Crystals is a down-to-earth, kindhearted, and ambitious individual whose energy is youthful and who appears confident and self-assured. Very often, their optimism and enthusiasm come from a place of innocence that has been nurtured by a strong support system or family who has sheltered them from disappointment, and they have yet to be subject to the burdens of the outside world. They thrive when learning new things, are extremely attentive to detail, and enjoy spending time exploring their own interests. More introverted than most, these types feel at peace when immersed in nature. Their patience and calm give them a keen sense of clarity, which prevents them from making hasty or impulsive decisions. A dedicated, determined person who has much to learn as they age.

QUESTIONS TO ASK

⚠ How can I be open to new opportunities in my life?

⚠ Are there new messages or projects being presented to me at this time?

REVERSED

When reversed, this could indicate an enthusiastic energy that is channeled into discussing future plans without enough action or organization to back these up. An emphasis on short-term rather than long-term goals. A need to calculate the necessary steps for achieving success.

KNIGHT OF CRYSTALS

Keys: committed • hardworking • conservative • detail oriented
• stubborn • nature lover

KNIGHT OF CRYSTALS

Standing here beneath a full moon, the Knight of Crystals has set his mind on the task in hand: working and harnessing the energy of a great crystal. He is skilled and adept in his craft and uses the powers of this element to his greatest advantage, rarely taking a moment to rest or pause. He has refined and mastered this ritual due to his years of experience and knows how to use his time wisely.

THE MESSAGE

It is time to take action! If the task ahead seems tedious or daunting, it is still important to remain focused and follow through. Once you do this, you will feel a renewed sense of accomplishment. Think of the rewards!

PEOPLE

The Knight of Crystals is an old soul. He has seen and experienced more than most and lives his life from a place of quiet, meditative wisdom. With strong views about the world, he has no time for rebellious irresponsibility or petulance from others. His ability to plan ahead and work long hours are key to his lifestyle: He does what needs to be done and reaps the benefits. A loyal and responsible person, the Knight of Crystals will always follow through on promises and plans and is very trustworthy, sharing his wisdom with those who seek his help. He is patient, levelheaded, and can think carefully in any situation. While he may not be the most adventurous type, he makes a loving friend and partner. He can, however, be overly cautious or conservative in his views, which may sometimes make him seem inflexible to others.

QUESTIONS TO ASK

△   How can I set my mind to the task ahead?

△   Are there any dreams or projects that I would like to focus on next?

REVERSED

A sense of boredom or restlessness. The current energy may be stagnant and will need to shift in order to make room for new opportunities. If there has been a resistance to change, now is the time to take constructive action. This card can also indicate someone nonspontaneous, who is set in their ways. A change in mindset may be needed.

QUEEN OF CRYSTALS

Keys: motherly • cautious • nurturing • loving • down-to-earth
• fertility • home

QUEEN OF CRYSTALS

Here, the beautiful Queen of Crystals sits in an earthly space, embodying an inner richness of spirit and love that radiates into the world around her. Before her is a collection of her most treasured crystals: energetic tools of healing that she freely shares with others. At her side rests a white tiger, her loving familiar who symbolizes her serene strength and calm demeanor. In the presence of these two, you are welcome, cherished, and nurtured.

THE MESSAGE

A time to be practical and resourceful with your plans. The building of a stable and realistic foundation. What steps will you take in order to remain healthy, happy, and secure in your life? Remember to be compassionate and kind to others.

PEOPLE

The Queen of Crystals is a warm and motherly individual who knows how to maintain a healthy and happy life. You will often find her balancing her commitments, responsibilities, relationships, and family duties simultaneously without breaking a sweat. She is a great nurturer and provider and goes above and beyond all expectation when it comes to taking care of others. Her deep connection to the earth is reflected in her own spiritual practice, whereby she sources wisdom and magic from the elements around her. From this higher awareness also comes a sense of security, which is often reflected in how she handles finances; she knows the true value of money lies beyond mere physical affluence, seeing it rather as a means to create a comfortable lifestyle for herself and her family. As she is extremely hardworking and pragmatic, she attracts others to her for her wisdom and support.

QUESTIONS TO ASK

⚠ How can I nurture my own hidden talents?

⚠ How can I find a greater sense of balance at this time?

REVERSED

A time to shift energetic blockages. A need for grounding and a detachment from materialistic views. A time to meditate on life goals. What is being taken for granted? Perhaps there is a need for security, whether financial or emotional.

KING OF CRYSTALS

Keys: business savvy • logical • family oriented • pragmatic
• reliable • supportive

KING OF CRYSTALS

Standing in a cosmic dreamscape, here the King of Crystals looks out into the light around him, feeling at peace with the life he has built. A mature wisdom radiates from his energy, as he has grown from experience and has learned to align with gratitude and love. Above his hands float the forms of seven sacred crystals, vessels of the wisdom, prosperity, and abundance that he has received through his own making.

THE MESSAGE

If you look to the future with a clear vision and move forward with self-discipline and determination, there is nothing you cannot accomplish. The King of Crystals reminds us to stay attentive to detail and to be open to new opportunities.

PEOPLE

The King of Crystals is a maverick who is extremely capable and ahead of the game. Being ambitious and dedicated, he is more often than not highly successful in his career. He has lived his life to the fullest and has refined his wisdom down to a keen sense of material stability, building a strong foundation of support for his family and loved ones. His pragmatism can provide you with clear and honest advice, as he is always willing to help those who ask for guidance or direction. The King of Crystals can sometimes appear shy or introverted, but do not be fooled by this exterior; underneath the surface, he is highly sensitive, with deep connections to both the earth and spirit world. He may also indicate someone who has the ability to sweep you off your feet and be a great romantic, or point to a person in a place of authority such as a mentor, a teacher, or a guide who will offer you a new direction or sound advice.

QUESTIONS TO ASK

⚠ How can I connect with my heart and dreams?

⚠ How can I harness and focus my energy to manifest my goals freely?

REVERSED

A rigid way of looking at the world. This card reversed may also indicate excess materialism or self-indulgence. Being blinded by frivolous things. A possessive or authoritative attitude. A desire for social status and recognition. A disconnection from one's Higher Self and spiritual nature.

THE AKASHIC RECORDS

Keys: collective information • universal consciousness
• connections • transformation

THE AKASHIC RECORDS

Unique to the Starchild Tarot, this 79th card represents the *Akasha* or Akashic Records. Traditionally identifying a great sky or heavenly realm, the Akashic Records have also been referred to as a "living library" or "The Book of Life," defining an etheric repository of the collective universal consciousness. The Akashic Records hold every thought, action, word, and emotion that has ever taken place; and, as so much is stored within its database, it is constantly changing and updating with new information, with each of us embodying a single note in its grand orchestra of energy.

THE MESSAGE

The Akashic Records are here to assist you in understanding the greater lessons you have come to learn and are a deeper resource for spiritual empowerment and transformation. When this card shows up, it comes as a reminder of the endless possibilities that are available to you. These insights can be accessed in various ways, including: past-life memories, intuitive glimpses, moments of déjà vu or epiphanies, prayer, loving connections with others, listening to music, enjoying dance and exercise, spending time in nature, being creative, and—above all—following your heart. We can also explore the Akashic Records through meditation, dreaming, and even by reading the Tarot. How you access your own Akashic Records will be specific to you, so trusting your intuition will be very helpful as you learn to access this universal tool. With time and practice, learning to work with the Akashic Records can be a magical and enlightening experience.

QUESTIONS TO ASK

⚠ How can I bond with my Higher Self?

⚠ What is my higher calling in life?

⚠ Which lessons am I here on Earth to learn?

REVERSED

This card has no reversed position.

TAROT SPREADS

This next step involves laying out your individual cards into the context and pattern of a Tarot spread. Here, you may create your own designs or follow the guided instructions of one that already exists. Spreads are collective arrangements of individual cards that shine light on certain topics or themes. Each card plays an important role within its specific individual placement as well as the broader collective energy of the Tarot spread. When we read a Tarot spread, we also observe and interpret the connection the cards have to one another.

To access a printout of these spreads, along with additional journal prompts, spiritual keys for the Major Arcana, and other Tarot exercises, please visit: **StarchildTarot.com**.

CHOOSING YOUR SIGNIFICATOR

Very often, readings and Tarot spreads may involve choosing a significator. This means selecting a card that represents you or the person for whom you are reading (the querent). This is a card that brings you (symbolically) into the context of the reading. You may choose one from the court cards, which typically include depictions of people, or perhaps from a Major Arcana key. When creating a Tarot spread of your own, it can be helpful to include an initial position for the significator, to deepen the reading from a more personal angle.

With the Celtic Cross Tarot spread that is included in this book, for example, very often the first card is set as the significator card. Each remaining card expands on and broadens the information of the reading from this center point of focus.

ONE-CARD DRAW

The one-card draw is a great way to gain some insight or a quick piece of advice. This can be done when you are asking a specific question, while meditating, or when you are focused on one specific theme. It is also a great way to start off your day! I like to do this when I first wake up and have a cup of coffee or when I am writing in my dream journal. This method is also helpful when you want to learn the individual card meanings, without the complexity of a spread.

THE MOON

THREE-CARD DRAW

This is a quick and simple spread that provides you with a well-rounded interpretation to any questions or concerns you may have. It is one of the most common layouts to use and can be modified in many different ways. It typically reveals past influences that may be exerting pressure on the present situation, the present matter at hand, along with any potential future energies that may show up.

You can also be creative with this one and come up with your own placements or expand from each design by adding the significator within each reading.

Here are some alternative draws that also may be used with the three-card spread:

situation • action • outcome
you • the other person • relationship
mind • body • spirit
weakness • strength • advice
dreams • challenges • advice
head • heart • soul
past life • present life • future life

ACE OF SWORDS

1

ACE OF CRYSTALS

2

NINE OF CRYSTALS

3

THE CELTIC CROSS SPREAD

The Celtic Cross is one of the most popular and versatile Tarot spreads that exist today. There are various placement options that may come with this design; however, the meanings are typically the same. This Tarot spread illuminates the energies and themes that are surrounding you or the situation at hand, offering an in-depth perspective for advice. You may begin this reading by first placing the significator card down to introduce your energy into the spread (or the person for whom you are reading) before beginning with step 1.

0. **The significator**
1. **The heart of the matter:** This covers you and highlights the immediate energies related to your question or concern.
2. **The challenge:** This crosses you and highlights any blocks or obstacles that may be in the way.
3. **The root:** This lies beneath you and highlights the rooted energies that are exerting forces or past influences into the present situation.
4. **The recent past:** This is behind you or in the process of passing.
5. **The best that can be achieved:** This crowns you and highlights the best that can come to pass from the situation.
6. **The immediate future:** This is before you and highlights new energies or circumstances that are nearing or coming into play.
7. **You and your power:** This describes your internal state, current attitudes, or strength within the context of the reading.
8. **External influences or forces:** This may highlight people, energies, or circumstances surrounding your situation.
9. **Your hopes and fears:** what you may be holding on to in terms of hopes or fears.
10. **The outcome:** the probable future.

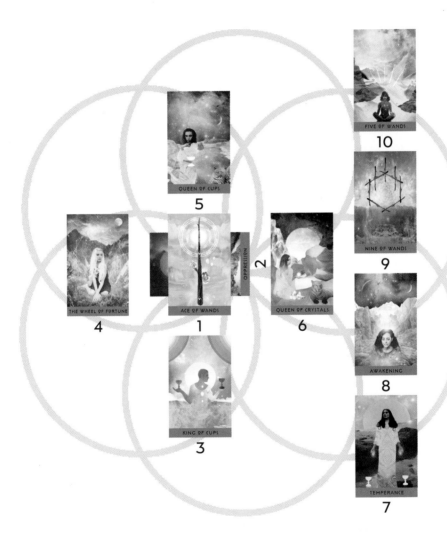

THE STARSEED SPREAD

The Starseed Spread is a quick and easy layout that works as an intuitive snapshot of our present circumstances. This can point toward internal energies, people, or forces that are surrounding you, and how you can go about navigating though any obstacles or challenges that may show up. It can also help you work with any new opportunities that are approaching, as a way to sustain a positive outcome for the future. Again, feel free to add a significator card before beginning this reading, and interpret the cards in whatever position suits you (upright or reversed).

1. **External forces or underlying situation:** who, what, where, when, how?
2. **The first step/initiator:** How or where do I begin?
3. **How to sustain yourself:** What do I need to do to support myself?
4. **What you need to learn:** What greater lesson is being presented to me?
5. **The outcome:** the culmination of energies.

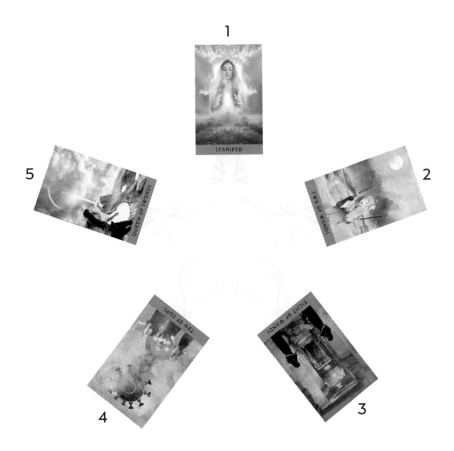

THE AKASHIC SPREAD

The Akashic spread is a deeply attuned layout that bridges beyond the past-present-future configurations of some designs. As a more spiritually inclined window, it looks into the multilayers of who we are, offering gentle yet practical advice. With the Akashic Records as its theme, it also works as a doorway into new realms of thought or inquiry in order to help us look at patterns or blockages that may need to be processed or released. From here, we may begin to unlock new insights and dreams that align with our Higher Self.

1. **My Higher Self:** What will be shared through clues, synchronicities, visions, or feelings? What is my higher calling?
2. **My current energies:** What do I need to process at this time? Where do I stand?
3. **Lower vibrations:** What do I need to release or let go of? What facets of my Shadow Self can I learn to integrate or process?
4. **Karmic imprints:** What am I still repeating? What lessons do I need to learn?
5. **Awakening:** Is there something greater that I am being drawn toward? What greater dreams are waiting for my awareness?

1

KNIGHT OF WANDS

4

ACE OF SWORDS

5

FIVE OF SWORDS

2

THREE OF WANDS

THE HIEROPHANT

3

THE HIGHER SELF—
SHADOW SPREAD

This spread takes a deeper look at our internal energies, forces, or underlying shadows, along with the sacred wisdom of our Higher Self.

Very often we think of the Shadow Self as something that exists as separate from our Higher Self; however, these two forces may often expand and contract in relation to one another, creating a symbiotic dance in our life. When we are able to take a deeper look into our restrained dreams, fears, pains, suppressions, desires, and repeated lessons, we have the potential to unlock new forms of wisdom and medicine that allow us to grow and transform, connecting with a higher awareness that nourishes our heart and soul. With these greater lessons come new awakenings, through the myriad of experiences that often cause us to fall, then rise. Without the dark, there is no light. Without the light, there is no dark.

With this spread, feel free to begin by first adding the significator card, then work from either the Shadow placements or the Higher Self level. As this is a very personal and intuitive spread, the interpretation will be specific to you, so taking notes can be helpful with this one. What does your inner voice tell you? How do the cards spark clues or thoughts related to your own life? What do you see in the images, and how do they relate to each placement and meaning for you?

THE HIGHER SELF

1. What sacred knowledge or awakenings should I be expecting soon?

2. What desires or outlets should I be exploring?

3. What do my guides want me to know at this time?

4. How can I nurture my spirit and dreams?

THE SHADOW SELF

1. What past influences (internal or external) are still exerting pressure on me?

2. What karmic patterns or lessons do I keep repeating?

3. Where is my shadow presenting itself the most in my life?

4. How can I learn to release my fears?

THE HIGHER SELF

THE SHADOW SELF

THE METATRON SPREAD

The Metatron spread offers a deep connection to our own spiritual gifts, lifetimes, and encoded wisdom. Metatron (also known as Thoth) was chosen as the theme for this layout because he is a celestial guide who has been known throughout the ages as the great scribe and recordkeeper of all that is contained in the Akashic Records and universal library. This repository of knowledge has also been described as the Book of Life, which is readily available for you to access and explore at your own pace. Archangel Metatron also helps us clear away any blockages or lower vibrational energies that may need to be released, creating space for new healing and energetic downloads.

In this spread, each card works harmoniously with the others, expanding from its previous message. This layout is also very effective when combined with premeditation, intention setting, or ritual, along with any journaling you may want to record as you interpret each card. What thoughts, visions, or insights come to you as you work through this process? Let this wisdom flow through you as you trust your inner voice.

1. **Celestial connection:** How can I access the higher realms of my consciousness? What card points toward this awakening?
2. **Akashic connection:** How can I activate my own spiritual gifts? What ancient wisdom am I ready to receive? What card helps reveal this lesson?
3. **Universal connection:** What encoded information from my past should I acknowledge? What card reveals the past life lessons that are still waiting for my awareness?
4. **Spirit-cosmic connection:** What do my guides or ancestors want me to know or learn?
5. **Soul Star connection:** What inner healing or clearing do I need to do in order to connect with my Higher Self or higher calling?
6. **Crown Chakra connection:** What new awakenings can be expected soon? What downloads am I receiving at this time?

7. **Third Eye connection:** How can I activate my own intuition and psychic abilities? Are there clearings or patterns that may need to be released beforehand? What card points toward the shadows that may be blocking my vision? What card points toward the gifts I need to tune into more?

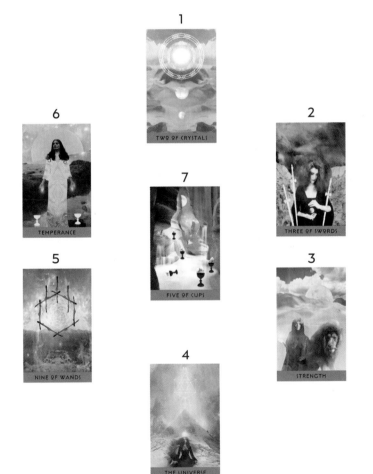

THE PYRAMID SPREAD

The Pyramid Spread is an intuitive exercise that allows you to play with the positions of the cards. You don't need to place them down in any particular order; instead, you may decide where you would like to begin, then go from there. Once you have completed the pyramid, take note of its overall construction. How do the cards work with one another? Are there particular suits or keys of the Major Arcana that stand out? What kind of a foundation have you built?

(Top card)

My Higher Self: What sacred knowledge am I ready to receive?

(Second row of cards)

Past: an active external or internal force that has affected my path.

Present: a force in my life that strengthens my light.

Future: an energy or situation to consider.

(Third row of cards)

Awakenings: What awakenings await me?

Desires: What desires or outlets should I explore?

Guides: What do my guides want me to know?

Love: How is love presenting itself in my life?

Shadow: What shadow work can I support?

MY HIGHER SELF

What sacred
knowledge
am I ready to
receive?

PAST

PRESENT

FUTURE

An active
external or
internal force
that has
affected my
path

A force in my
life that
strengthens
my light

An energy or
situation to
consider

AWAKENINGS

DESIRES

GUIDES

LOVE

SHADOW

What
awakenings
await me?

What desires
or outlets
should I
explore?

What do my
guides want
me to know?

How is love
presenting
itself in my life?

What shadow
work can I
support?

ACKNOWLEDGMENTS

To my beloved King of Crystals, Sterling. You are the light and love of my life. Thank you for your constant unconditional support. I treasure our soul connection beyond lifetimes and words. *Te adoro*. To the soul sisters of my Tarot deck who are also the Queens of my life: Sylvia Mercedes Tennant, Ali Vanstolk, Kelsey Bjur, Richelle Elizabeth Newson, Candy Lefrancois, Carla Sandfort. Thank you for being the best muses anyone could ask for.

Special thanks to the Penguin Random House UK team: to Laura Horsley and Laura Higginson, my incredible commissioning editors who gave me so much support and sound wisdom throughout the creation of this book; Annabel Wright, Molly Powell, and Clare Thorpe from whitefox, for your beautiful design work and support; my editor, Sue Lascelles, for imparting your wisdom and believing in the Tarot. And deepest gratitude to Melissa Rhodes, Holly Swayne, and the entire team at Andrews McMeel for their invaluable help with the U.S. edition of the book.

To my wonderful parents; my brother, Stephen; and my darling cousin, Ashley—thank you for standing by me throughout all of my chapters and quirky moments. To my mother-in-law (love), Elizabeth, who taught me to be strong and true at every corner and turn. Love and gratitude to my dear Trevor Ayerst and Nathan Krause for walking this life with me as true believers in magic. My world is so much brighter with you both.

And, finally, to my Starchild readers. This is for you.

MODEL CREDITS

Below is a complete list of the incredible models featured throughout this book and the Starchild Tarot. Many of them are intuitive healers, teachers, readers, and spiritual guides. They have added a truly remarkable energy to these pages. Thank you all from the bottom of my heart!

Pages 24 and 122—Kelsey Bjur (@spiral.circle); 26, 44, 108, 116, and 146—Miranda Hedman; 28—Briana Luna (thehoodwitch.com); 30—Sylvia Mercedes Tennant (@zaleskajewelry); 34 and 148—Jessica Lansfield; 36—Innis Wolf and Ali VanStolk; 40 and 134—Sophia Knapp (@tarotbysophia), taken by Robb Schlage; 42—Candy Lefrancois; 46—Jenny Larson; 48—Maryam Hasnaa (@vibrationalmedicine); 50—Janna Prosvirina; 52—Segovia Amil; 56 and 140—Stephanie G. Bauman; 60, 66, and 118—Georgia Waters; 64—Rachael Webb (@soulstarmedicine), taken by In Her Image Photography; 74—Sarah Robison; 138—Carla Sandfort; 82—Brittny Nicole Soto; 84—Janna Prosvirina, taken by Kuoma (deviantart.com); 86 and 176—Kristen (@youareluminous); 90—Marti Ragan, taken by Felicia van Ham; 94—Nathan Krause; 96—Leah Hoffman (@leahhoffff); 98—Matt Harris (@mph4586); 104—Mirvilina; 112—Ruby Scott; 124—Mahia Keepa-Hale, taken by Cathleen Tarawhiti; 126—Millana Snow (@millanasnow), taken by Joseph Paradiso; 128—Andrew Wiggill; 136—J'aimeclaire Victoria Rose Boland; 142 and 154—Jessica Truscott; 152 and 174—Olivia Mavis Walker; 156—Julia Maximo Ferrari; 158—Francis Eadie; 166—Phoebe Dykstra (@phoebedykstra); 168—Stephen Noel; 172—Christie-Leigh Williams, taken by Cathleen Tarawhiti; 178—Natalia Benson (@natalia_benson), taken by Tiffanie Byron (@tiffaniebyron); 182—Ali VanStolk; 184—Trevor Ayerst; 186—Richelle Elizabeth Newson (@RocoNewson); 188—Sterling Holland-Roy.

Website: starchildtarot.com   **Facebook:** facebook.com/starchildtarot
Instagram: instagram.com/starchildtarot   **Email:** info@starchildtarot.com